SUMMER KNOWLEDGE

New and Selected Poems
1938–1958

Summer

Knowledge

NEW AND SELECTED POEMS

1938–1958

by

Delmore

Schwartz

1959

DOUBLEDAY & COMPANY, INC.

GARDEN CITY, NEW YORK

The poems "The Dark and Falling Summer," "Vivaldi," "During December's Death," and "A Little Morning Music" appeared originally in *The New Yorker*, copyright © 1958, 1959 by The New Yorker Magazine, Inc. The poems "Fulfillment" and "Seurat's Sunday Afternoon Along the Seine" appeared originally in *Art News*. The following poems, which appeared in *Vaudeville for a Princess*, are reprinted by permission of New Directions: "The Winter Twilight, Glowing Black and Gold," "I Did Not Know the Spoils of Joy," and "Starlight Like Intuition Pierced the Twelve," copyright 1950 by New Directions, and "Lincoln" from *Genesis I*, copyright 1943 by New Directions. The section "The Dream of Knowledge" in this book is from *In Dreams Begin Responsibilities*, copyright 1938 by New Directions. "A Small Score" and "How Strange Love Is, in Every State of Consciousness" appeared in *Mutiny* under the titles "A Little Morning Music" and "Praise of Creation."

Library of Congress Catalog Card Number 59–10689
Copyright © 1954, 1955, 1958, 1959 by Delmore Schwartz
Copyright 1959 by Modern Poetry Association
Copyright 1959 by Harrison-Blaine, Inc.
All Rights Reserved
Printed in the United States of America
Designed by Diana Klemin
First Edition

To John Crowe Ransom and Dwight Macdonald

AUTHOR'S NOTE

Most of the poems in the first half of the book have been revised since they were first published in 1938. I have also included several poems written at that time but never published before. The second half of the book consists of a selection of poems written during the past five years and, in addition, several poems selected from *Vaudeville for a Princess* and one poem from *Genesis: Book One*, a long narrative poem which appeared in 1943. Thus, in a very real sense, all of the poems in this volume are selected poems; and, since for me, as for many poets, the temptation to revise one's work is often irresistible, there is also a sense in which all of the poems in this selection are new: I have not always included various revisions, but I have examined and chosen among them from the point of view which is signified by the title of the volume: *Summer Knowledge.*

Every point of view, every kind of knowledge and every kind of experience is limited and ignorant; nevertheless, so far as I know, this volume seems to me to be as representative as it could be. I would have included much, but not all, of the poetry I have written, published, and revised during the past twenty years if this volume were a collection rather than a selection consisting of new and selected poems.

D. S.

April 1959

CONTENTS

I

THE DREAM OF KNOWLEDGE

1

The Dreams Which Begin in Responsibilities

2

The Repetitive Heart:

POEMS IN IMITATION OF THE FUGUE

13

5

Morning Bells

6

The Kingdom of Poetry

Narcissus

I

The Dream
of
Knowledge

1

THE DREAMS
WHICH BEGIN
IN
RESPONSIBILITIES

The Ballad of the Children of the Czar

1

The children of the Czar
Played with a bouncing ball

In the May morning, in the Czar's garden,
Tossing it back and forth.

It fell among the flowerbeds
Or fled to the north gate.

A daylight moon hung up
In the Western sky, bald white.

Like Papa's face, said Sister,
Hurling the white ball forth.

2

While I ate a baked potato
Six thousand miles apart,

In Brooklyn, in 1916,
Aged two, irrational.

When Franklin D. Roosevelt
Was an Arrow Collar ad.

O Nicholas! Alas! Alas!
My grandfather coughed in your army,

Hid in a wine-stinking barrel,
For three days in Bucharest

Then left for America
To become a king himself.

3

I am my father's father,
You are your children's guilt.

In history's pity and terror
The child is Aeneas again;

Troy is in the nursery,
The rocking horse is on fire.

Child labor! The child must carry
His fathers on his back.

But seeing that so much is past
And that history has no ruth

For the individual,
Who drinks tea, who catches cold,

Let anger be general:
I hate an abstract thing.

4

Brother and sister bounced
The bounding, unbroken ball,

The shattering sun fell down
Like swords upon their play,

Moving eastward among the stars
Toward February and October.

But the Maywind brushed their cheeks
Like a mother watching sleep,

And if for a moment they fight
Over the bouncing ball

And sister pinches brother
And brother kicks her shins,

Well! The heart of man is known:
It is a cactus bloom.

5

The ground on which the ball bounces
Is another bouncing ball.

The wheeling, whirling world
Makes no will glad.

Spinning in its spotlight darkness,
It is too big for their hands.

A pitiless, purposeless Thing,
Arbitrary and unspent,

Made for no play, for no children,
But chasing only itself.

The innocent are overtaken,
They are not innocent.

They are their father's fathers,
The past is inevitable.

6

Now, in another October
Of this tragic star,

I see my second year,
I eat my baked potato.

It is my buttered world,
But, poked by my unlearned hand,

It falls from the highchair down
And I begin to howl.

And I see the ball roll under
The iron gate which is locked.

Sister is screaming, brother is howling,
The ball has evaded their will.

Even a bouncing ball
Is uncontrollable,

And is under the garden wall.
I am overtaken by terror

Thinking of my father's fathers,
And of my own will.

In the Naked Bed, in Plato's Cave

In the naked bed, in Plato's cave,
Reflected headlights slowly slid the wall,
Carpenters hammered under the shaded window,
Wind troubled the window curtains all night long,
A fleet of trucks strained uphill, grinding,
Their freights covered, as usual.
The ceiling lightened again, the slanting diagram
Slid slowly forth.
            Hearing the milkman's chop,
His striving up the stair, the bottle's chink,
I rose from bed, lit a cigarette,
And walked to the window. The stony street
Displayed the stillness in which buildings stand,
The street-lamp's vigil and the horse's patience.
The winter sky's pure capital
Turned me back to bed with exhausted eyes.

Strangeness grew in the motionless air. The loose
Film grayed. Shaking wagons, hooves' waterfalls,
Sounded far off, increasing, louder and nearer.
A car coughed, starting. Morning, softly
Melting the air, lifted the half-covered chair
From underseas, kindled the looking-glass,
Distinguished the dresser and the white wall.
The bird called tentatively, whistled, called,
Bubbled and whistled, so! Perplexed, still wet
With sleep, affectionate, hungry and cold. So, so,
O son of man, the ignorant night, the travail
Of early morning, the mystery of beginning
Again and again,
            while History is unforgiven.

Some who are uncertain compel me. They fear
The Ace of Spades. They fear
Love offered suddenly, turning from the mantelpiece,
Sweet with decision. And they distrust
The fireworks by the lakeside, first the spuft,
Then the colored lights, rising.
Tentative, hesitant, doubtful, they consume
Greedily Caesar at the prow returning,
Locked in the stone of his act and office.
While the brass band brightly bursts over the water
They stand in the crowd lining the shore
Aware of the water beneath Him. They know it. Their eyes
Are haunted by water.

Disturb me, compel me. It is not true
That "no man is happy," but that is not
The sense which guides you. If we are
Unfinished (we are, unless hope is a bad dream),
You are exact. You tug my sleeve
Before I speak, with a shadow's friendship,
And I remember that we who move
Are moved by clouds that darken midnight.

The Beautiful American Word, Sure

The beautiful American word, Sure,
As I have come into a room, and touch
The lamp's button, and the light blooms with such
Certainty where the darkness loomed before,

As I care for what I do not know, and care
Knowing for little she might not have been,
And for how little she would be unseen,
The intercourse of lives miraculous and dear.

Where the light is, and each thing clear,
Separate from all others, standing in its place,
I drink the time and touch whatever's near,

And hope for day when the whole world has that face:
For what assures her present every year?
In dark accidents the mind's sufficient grace.

O *Love, Sweet Animal*

O Love, dark animal,
With your strangeness go
Like any freak or clown:
Appease the child in her
Because she is alone
Many years ago
Terrified by a look
Which was not meant for her.
Brush your heavy fur
Against her, long and slow
Stare at her like a book,
Her interests being such
No one can look too much.
Tell her how you know
Nothing can be taken
Which has not been given:
For you time is forgiven:
Informed by hell and heaven
You are not mistaken.

Father and Son

"From a certain point onward there is no longer any turning back. That is the point that must be reached."

FRANZ KAFKA

Father:
On these occasions, the feelings surprise,
Spontaneous as rain, and they compel
Explicitness, embarrassed eyes——

Son:
Father, you're not Polonius, you're reticent,
But sure. I can already tell
The unction and falsetto of the sentiment
Which gratifies the facile mouth, but springs
From no felt, had, and wholly known things.

Father:
You must let me tell you what you fear
When you wake up from sleep, still drunk with sleep:
You are afraid of time and its slow drip,
Like melting ice, like smoke upon the air
In February's glittering sunny day.
Your guilt is nameless, because its name is time,
Because its name is death. But you can stop
Time as it dribbles from you, drop by drop.

Son:
But I thought time was full of promises,
Even as now, the emotion of going away——

Father:
That is the first of all its menaces,
The lure of a future different from today;
All of us always are turning away
To the cinema and Asia. All of us go
To one indeterminate nothing.

Son:

Must it be so?
I question the sentiment you give to me,
As premature, not to be given, learned alone
When experience shrinks upon the chilling bone.
I would be sudden now and rash in joy,
As if I lived forever, the future my toy.
Time is a dancing fire at twenty-one,
Singing and shouting and drinking to the sun,
Powerful at the wheel of a motor-car,
Not thinking of death which is foreign and far.

Father:
If time flowed from your will and were a feast
I would be wrong to question your zest.
But each age betrays the same weak shape.
Each moment is dying. You will try to escape
From melting time and your dissipating soul
By hiding your head in a warm and dark hole.
See the evasions which so many don,
To flee the guilt of time they become one,
That is, the one number among masses,
The one anonymous in the audience,
The one expressionless in the subway,
In the subway evening among so many faces,
The one who reads the daily newspaper,
Separate from actor and act, a member

Of public opinion, never involved.
Integrated in the revery of a fine cigar,
Fleeing to childhood at the symphony concert,
Buying sleep at the drugstore, grandeur
At the band concert, Hawaii
On the screen, and everywhere a specious splendor:
One, when he is sad, has something to eat,
An ice cream soda, a toasted sandwich,
Or has his teeth fixed, but can always retreat
From the actual pain, and dream of the rich.
This is what one does, what one becomes
Because one is afraid to be alone,
Each with his own death in the lonely room.
But there is a stay. You can stop
Time as it dribbles from you, drop by drop.

Son:
Now I am afraid. What is there to be known?

Father:
Guilt, guilt of time, nameless guilt.
Grasp firmly your fear, thus grasping your self,
Your actual will. Stand in mastery,
Keeping time in you, its terrifying mystery.
Face yourself, constantly go back
To what you were, your own history.
You are always in debt. Do not forget
The dream postponed which would not quickly get
Pleasure immediate as drink, but takes
The travail of building, patience with means.
See the wart on your face and on your friend's face,
On your friend's face and indeed on your own face.
The loveliest woman sweats, the animal stains
The ideal which is with us like the sky . . .

31

Son:
Because of that, some laugh, and others cry.

Father:
Do not look past and turn away your face.
You cannot depart and take another name,
Nor go to sleep with lies. Always the same,
Always the same self from the ashes of sleep
Returns with its memories, always, always,
The phoenix with eight hundred thousand memories!

Son:
What must I do that is most difficult?

Father:
You must meet your death face to face,
You must, like one in an old play,
Decide, once for all, your heart's place.
Love, power, and fame stand on an absolute
Under the formless night and the brilliant day,
The searching violin, the piercing flute.
Absolute! Venus and Caesar fade at that edge,
Hanging from the fiftieth-story ledge,
Or diminished in bed when the nurse presses
Her sickening unguents and her cold compresses.
When the news is certain, surpassing fear,
You touch the wound, the priceless, the most dear.
There in death's shadow, you comprehend
The irreducible wish, world without end.

Son:
I begin to understand the reason for evasion,
I cannot partake of your difficult vision.

32

Father:
Begin to understand the first decision.
Hamlet is the example; only dying
Did he take up his manhood, the dead's burden,
Done with evasion, done with sighing,
Done with revery.
                              Decide that you are dying
Because time is in you, ineluctable
As shadow, named by no syllable.
Act in that shadow, as if death were now:
Your own self acts then, then you know.

Son:
My father has taught me to be serious.

Father:
Be guilty of yourself in the full looking-glass.

Far Rockaway

"the cure of souls." HENRY JAMES

The radiant soda of the seashore fashions
Fun, foam, and freedom. The sea laves
The shaven sand. And the light sways forward
On the self-destroying waves.

The rigor of the weekday is cast aside with shoes,
With business suits and the traffic's motion;
The lolling man lies with the passionate sun,
Or is drunken in the ocean.

A socialist health takes hold of the adult,
He is stripped of his class in the bathing-suit,
He returns to the children digging at summer,
A melon-like fruit.

O glittering and rocking and bursting and blue
—Eternities of sea and sky shadow no pleasure:
Time unheard moves and the heart of man is eaten
Consummately at leisure.

The novelist tangential on the boardwalk overhead
Seeks his cure of souls in his own anxious gaze.
"Here," he says, "With whom?" he asks, "This?" he questions,
"What tedium, what blaze?"

"What satisfaction, fruit? What transit, heaven?
Criminal? justified? arrived at what June?"
That nervous conscience amid the concessions
Is a haunting, haunted moon.

The Sin of Hamlet

The horns in the harbor booming, vaguely,
Fog, forgotten, yesterday, conclusion,
Nostalgic, noising dim sorrow, calling
To sleep is it? I think so, and childhood,
Not the door opened and the stair descended,
The voice answered, the choice announced, the
Trigger touched in sharp declaration!

And when it comes, escape is small; the door
Creaks; the worms of fear spread veins; the furtive
Fugitive, looking backward, sees his
Ghost in the mirror, his shameful eyes, his mouth diseased.

When from the watercolored window idly you look
Each is but each and clear to see, not steep:
So does the neat print in an actual book
Marching as if to true conclusion, reap
The illimitable blue immensely overhead,
The night of the living and the day of the dead.

I drive in an auto all night long to reach
The apple which has sewed the sunlight up:
My simple self is nothing but the speech
Pleading for the overflow of that great cup,
The darkened body, the mind still as a frieze:
All else is merely means as complex as disease!

Someone Is Harshly Coughing as Before

Someone is harshly coughing on the next floor,
Sudden excitement catching the flesh of his throat:
Who is the sick one?
                    Who will knock at the door,
Ask what is wrong and sweetly pay attention,
The shy withdrawal of the sensitive face
Embarrassing both, but double shame is tender
—We will mind our ignorant business, keep our place.

But it is God, who has caught cold again,
Wandering helplessly in the world once more,
Now he is phthisic, and he is, poor Keats
(Pardon, O Father, unknowable Dear, this word,
Only the cartoon is lucid, only the curse is heard),
Longing for Eden, afraid of the coming war.

The past, a giant shadow like the twilight,
The moving street on which the autos slide,
The buildings' heights, like broken teeth,
Repeat necessity on every side,
The age requires death and is not denied,
He has come as a young man to be hanged once more!

Another mystery must be crucified,
Another exile bare his complex care,
Another spent head spill its wine, before
(When smoke in silence curves
                              from every fallen side)
Pity and Peace return, padding the broken floor
With heavy feet.
                  Their linen hands will hide
In the stupid opiate the exhausted war.

Tired and Unhappy, You Think of Houses

Tired and unhappy, you think of houses
Soft-carpeted and warm in the December evening,
While snow's white pieces fall past the window,
And the orange firelight leaps.
                                        A young girl sings
That song of Gluck where Orpheus pleads with Death;
Her elders watch, nodding their happiness
To see time fresh again in her self-conscious eyes:
The servants bring the coffee, the children retire,
Elder and younger yawn and go to bed,
The coals fade and glow, rose and ashen,
It is time to shake yourself! and break this
Banal dream, and turn your head
Where the underground is charged, where the weight
Of the lean buildings is seen,
Where close in the subway rush, anonymous
In the audience, well-dressed or mean,
So many surround you, ringing your fate,
Caught in an anger exact as a machine!

In the slight ripple, the fishes dart
Like fingers, centrifugal, like wishes
Wanton. And pleasures rise
                              as the eyes fall
Through the lucid water. The small pebble,
The clear clay bottom, the white shell
Are apparent, though superficial.
Who would ask more of the August afternoon?
Who would dig mines and follow shadows?
"I would," answers bored Heart, "Lounger, rise"
(Underlip trembling, face white with stony anger),
"The old error, the thought of sitting still,
"The senses drinking, by the summer river,
"On the tended lawn, below the traffic,
"As if time would pause,
                              and afternoon stay.
"No, night comes soon,
"With its cold mountains, with desolation,
                              unless Love build its city."

Concerning the Synthetic Unity of Apperception

"Trash, trash!" the king my uncle said,
"The spirit's smoke and weak as smoke ascends.

"Sit in the sun and not among the dead,
"Eat oranges! Pish tosh! The car attends.

"All ghosts come back. They do not like it there,
"No silky water and no big brown bear,

"No beer and no siestas up above."
"Uncle," I said, "I'm lonely. What is love?"

This drove him quite insane. Now he must knit
Time with apperception, bit by tiny bit.

Parlez-Vous Français?

Caesar, the amplifier voice, announces
Crime and reparation. In the barber shop
Recumbent men attend, while absently
The barber doffs the naked face with cream.
Caesar proposes, Caesar promises
Pride, justice, and the sun
Brilliant and strong on everyone,
Speeding one hundred miles an hour across the land:
Caesar declares the will. The barber firmly
Planes the stubble with a steady hand,
While all in barber chairs reclining,
In wet white faces, fully understand
Good and evil, who is Gentile, weakness and command.

And now who enters quietly? Who is this one
Shy, pale, and quite abstracted? Who is he?
It is the writer merely, with a three-day beard,
His tiredness not evident. He wears no tie.
And now he hears his enemy and trembles,
Resolving, speaks: "Écoutez! La plupart des hommes
Vivent des vies de désespoir silencieux,
Victimes des intentions innombrables. Et ça
Cet homme sait bien. Les mots de cette voix sont
Des songes et des mensonges. Il prend le choix,
Il prend la volonté, il porte la fin d'été,
La guerre. Écoutez-moi! Il porte la mort."
He stands there speaking and they laugh to hear
Rage and excitement from the foreigner.

By Circumstances Fed

By circumstances fed
Which divide attention
Among the living and the dead,
Under the blooms of the blossoming sun,
The gaze which is a tower towers
Day and night, hour by hour,
Critical of all and of one,
Dissatisfied with every flower
With all that's been done or undone,
Converting every feature
Into its own and unknown nature;
So, once in the drugstore,
Amid all the poppy, salve and ointment,
I suddenly saw, estranged there,
Beyond all disappointment,
My own face in the mirror.

A Young Child and His Pregnant Mother

At four years Nature is mountainous,
Mysterious, and submarine. Even

A city child knows this, hearing the subway's
Rumor underground. Between the grate,

Dropping his penny, he learned out all loss,
The irretrievable cent of fate,

And now this newest of the mysteries,
Confronts his honest and his studious eyes——

His mother much too fat and absentminded,
Gazing far past his face, careless of him,

His fume, his charm, his bedtime, and warm milk,
As soon the night will be too dark, the spring

Too late, desire strange, and time too fast,
This first estrangement is a gradual thing

(His mother once so svelte, so often sick!
Towering father did this: what a trick!)

Explained too cautiously, containing fear,
Another being's being, becoming dear:

All men are enemies: thus even brothers
Can separate each other from their mothers!

No better example than this unborn brother
Shall teach him of his exile from his mother,

Measured by his distance from the sky,
Spoken in two vowels,
                    I am I.

Prothalamion

"little soul, little flirting,
   little perverse one
      where are you off to now?
little wan one, firm one
   little exposed one . . .
      and never make fun of me again."

Now I must betray myself.
The feast of bondage and unity is near,
And none engaged in that great piety
When each bows to the other, kneels, and takes
Hand and hand, glance and glance, care and care,
None may wear masks or enigmatic clothes,
For weakness blinds the wounded face enough.
In this sense, see my shocking nakedness.

I gave a girl an apple when five years old,
Saying, Will you be sorry when I am gone?
Ravenous for such courtesies, my name
Is fed like a raving fire, insatiate still.
But do not be afraid.
For I forget myself. I do indeed
Before each genuine beauty, and I will
Forget myself before your unknown heart.

I will forget the speech my mother made
In a restaurant, trapping my father there
At dinner with his whore. Her spoken rage
Struck down the child of seven years
With shame for all three, with pity for
The helpless harried waiter, with anger for
The diners gazing, avid, and contempt,
And great disgust for every human being.
I will remember this. My mother's rhetoric
Has charmed my various tongue, but now I know
Love's metric seeks a rhyme more pure and sure.

For thus it is that I betray myself,
Passing the terror of childhood at second hand
Through nervous, learned fingertips.
At thirteen when a little girl died,
I walked for three weeks neither alive nor dead,
And could not understand and still cannot
The adult blind to the nearness of the dead,
Or carefully ignorant of their own death.
—This sense could shadow all time's curving fruits,
But we will taste of them the whole night long,
Forgetting no twelfth night, no fete of June,
But in the daylight knowing our nothingness.

Let Freud and Marx be wedding guests indeed!
Let them mark out the masks that face us there,
For of all anguish, weakness, loss and failure,
No form is cruel as self-deception, none
Shows day-by-day a bad dream long lived
And unbroken like the lies
We tell each other because we are rich or poor.
Though from the general guilt not free
We can keep honor by being poor.

The waste, the evil, the abomination
Is interrupted. The perfect stars persist
Small in the guilty night,
                            and Mozart shows
The irreducible incorruptible good
Risen past birth and death, though he is dead.
Hope, like a face reflected on the windowpane,
Remote and dim, fosters a myth or dream,
And in that dream, I speak, I summon all
Who are our friends somehow and thus I say:

"Bid the jewellers come with monocles,
Exclaiming, Pure! Intrinsic! Final!
Summon the children eating ice cream
To speak the chill thrill of immediacy.
Call for the acrobats who tumble
The ecstasy of the somersault.

Bid the self-sufficient stars be piercing
In the sublime and inexhaustible blue.

"Bring a mathematician, there is much to count,
The unending continuum of my attention:
Infinity will hurry his multiplied voice!
Bring the poised impeccable diver,
Summon the skater, precise in figure,
He knows the peril of circumstance,
The risk of movement and the hard ground.
Summon the florist! And the tobacconist!
All who have known a plant-like beauty:
Summon the charming bird for ignorant song.

"You, Athena, with your tired beauty,
Will you give me away? For you must come
In a bathing suit with that white owl
Whom, as I walk, I will hold in my hand.
You too, Crusoe, to utter the emotion
Of finding Friday, no longer alone;
You too, Chaplin, muse of the curbstone,
Mummer of hope, you understand!"

But this is fantastic and pitiful,
And no one comes, none will, we are alone,
And what is possible is my own voice,
Speaking its wish, despite its lasting fear;
Speaking its hope, its promise and its fear
The voice drunk with itself and rapt in fear,
Exaggeration, braggadocio,
Rhetoric and hope, and always fear:

"For fifty-six or for a thousand years,
I will live with you and be your friend,
And what your body and what your spirit bears
I will like my own body cure and tend.
But you are heavy and my body's weight
Is great and heavy: when I carry you
I lift upon my back time like a fate
Near as my heart, dark when I marry you.

"The voice's promise is easy, and hope
Is drunk, and wanton, and unwilled;
In time's quicksilver, where our desires grope,
The dream is warped or monstrously fulfilled.
In this sense, listen, listen, and draw near:
Love is inexhaustible and full of fear."

This life is endless and my eyes are tired,
So that, again and again, I touch a chair,
Or go to the window, press my face
Against it, hoping with substantial touch,
Colorful sight, or turning things to gain once more
The look of actuality, the certainty
Of those who run down stairs and drive a car.
Then let us be each other's truth, let us
Affirm the other's self, and be
The other's audience, the other's state,
Each to the other his sonorous fame.

Now you will be afraid, when, waking up,
Before familiar morning, by my mute side
Wan and abandoned then, when, waking up,
You see the lion or lamb upon my face
Or see the daemon breathing heavily
His sense of ignorance, his wish to die,
For I am nothing because my circus self
Divides its love a million times.

I am the octopus in love with God,
For thus is my desire inconclusible,
Until my mind, deranged in swimming tubes,
Issues its own darkness, clutching seas
—O God of my perfect ignorance,
Bring the New Year to my only sister soon,
Take from me strength and power to bless her head,
Give her the magnitude of secular trust,
Until she turns to me in her troubled sleep,
Seeing me in my wish, free from self-wrongs.

48

Faust in Old Age

"Poet and veteran of childhood, look!
See in me the obscene, for you have love,

For you have hatred, you, you must be judge,
Deliver judgement, Delmore Schwartz.

Well-known wishes have been to war.
The vicious mouth has chewed the vine.

The patient crab beneath the shirt
Has churned such interests as Indies meant.

For I have walked within and seen each sea,
The fish that flies, the broken burning bird,

Born again, beginning again, my breast!
Purple with persons like a tragic play.

For I have flown the cloud and fallen down,
Plucked Venus, sneering at her moan.

I took the train that takes away remorse;
I cast down every king like Socrates.

I knocked each nut to find the meat;
A worm was there and not a mint.

Metaphysicians could have told me this,
But each learns for himself, as in the kiss.

Polonius I poked, not him
To whom aspires spire and hymn,

Who succours children and the very poor;
I pierced the pompous Premier, not Jesus Christ,

I pricked Polonius, and Moby Dick,
The ego bloomed into an octopus.

Now come I to the exhausted West at last;
I know my vanity, my nothingness,

Now I float will-less in despair's dead sea,
Every man my enemy.

Spontaneous, I have too much to say,
And what I say will no one not old see:

If we could love one another, it would be well. But as it is, I am
sorry for the whole world, myself apart. My heart is full of memory
and desire, and in its last nervousness, there is pity for those I have
touched, but only hatred and contempt for myself."

Sonnet:
The Ghosts of James and Peirce in Harvard Yard

In memory of D. W. Prall

The ghosts of James and Peirce in Harvard Yard
At star-pierced midnight, after the chapel bell
(Episcopalian! palian! the ringing soared!)
Stare at me now as if they wished me well.
In the waking dream amid the trees which fall,
Bar and bough of shadow, by my shadow crossed,
They have not slept for long and they know all,
Know time's exhaustion and the spirit's cost.

"We studied the radiant sun, the star's pure seed:
Darkness is infinite! The blind can see
Hatred's necessity and love's grave need
Now that the poor are murdered across the sea,
And you are ignorant, who hear the bell;
Ignorant, you walk between heaven and hell."

Sonnet:
O City, City

To live between terms, to live where death
Has his loud picture in the subway ride,
Being amid six million souls, their breath
An empty song suppressed on every side,
Where the sliding auto's catastrophe
Is a gust past the curb, where numb and high
The office building rises to its tyranny,
Is our anguished diminution until we die.

Whence, if ever, shall come the actuality
Of a voice speaking the mind's knowing,
The sunlight bright on the green windowshade,
And the self articulate, affectionate, and flowing,
Ease, warmth, light, the utter showing,
When in the white bed all things are made.

What Is To Be Given

What is to be given,
Is spirit, yet animal,
Colored, like heaven,
Blue, yellow, beautiful.

The blood is checkered by
So many stains and wishes,
Between it and the sky
You could not choose, for riches.

Yet let me now be careful
Not to give too much
To one so shy and fearful
For like a gun is touch.

For the One Who Would Take Man's Life in His Hands

Tiger Christ unsheathed his sword,
Threw it down, became a lamb.
Swift spat upon the species, but
Took two women to his heart.
Samson who was strong as death
Paid his strength to kiss a slut.
Othello that stiff warrior
Was broken by a woman's heart.
Troy burned for a sea-tax, also for
Possession of a charming whore.
What do all examples show?
What must the finished murderer know?

You cannot sit on bayonets,
Nor can you eat among the dead.
When all are killed, you are alone,
A vacuum comes where hate has fed.
Murder's fruit is silent stone,
The gun increases poverty.
With what do these examples shine?
The soldier turned to girls and wine.
Love is the tact of every good,
The only warmth, the only peace.

"What have I said?" asked Socrates,
"Affirmed extremes, cried yes and no,
Taken all parts, denied myself,
Praised the caress, extolled the blow,
Soldier and lover quite deranged
Until their motions are exchanged.
—What do all examples show?
What can any actor know?
The contradiction in every act,
The infinite task of the human heart."

For the One Who Would Not Take His Life in His Hands

Athlete, virtuoso,
Training for happiness,
Bend arm and knee, and seek
The body's sharp distress,
For pain is pleasure's cost,
Denial is the route
To speech before the millions
Or personal with the flute.

The ape and great Achilles,
Heavy with their fate,
Batter doors down, strike
Small children at the gate,
Driven by love to this,
As knock-kneed Hegel said,
To seek with a sword their peace,
That the child may be taken away
From the hurly-burly and fed.

Ladies and Gentlemen, said
The curious Socrates,
I have asked, What is this life
But a childermass,
As Abraham recognized,
A working with the knife
At animal, maid and stone
Until we have cut down
All but the soul alone:
Through hate we guard our love,
And its distinction's known.

Saint, revolutionist,
God and sage know well,
That there is a place
Where that much-rung bell,
The well-beloved body,
And its sensitive face
Must be sacrificed.

There is, it seems, in this
A something meaningless,
Hanging without support
And yet too dear to touch,
That life should seek its end
Where no will can descend,
Facing a gun to see
Long actuality.

What is this that is
The good of nothingness,
The death of Socrates
And that strange man on the cross
Seeking out all loss?
For men love life until
It shames both face and will.

Neither in hell nor heaven
Is the answer given,
Both are a servant's pay:
But they wish to know
How far the will can go,
Lest their infinite play
And their desires be
Shadow and mockery.

Cambridge, Spring 1937

At last the air fragrant, the bird's bubbling whistle
Succinct in the unknown unsettled trees:
O little Charles, beside the Georgian colleges
And milltown New England; at last the wind soft,
The sky unmoving, and the dead look
Of factory windows separate, at last,
From wind gray and wet:
                                    for now the sunlight
Thrashes its wet shellac on brickwalk and gutter,
White splinters streak midmorning and doorstep,
Winter passes as the lighted streetcar
Moves at midnight, one scene of the past,
Droll and unreal, stiff, stilted and hooded.

Socrates' ghost must haunt me now,
Notorious death has let him go,
He comes to me with a clumsy bow,
Saying in his disused voice,
That I do not know I do not know,
The mechanical whims of appetite
Are all that I have of conscious choice,
The butterfly caged in electric light
Is my only day in the world's great night,
Love is not love, it is a child
Sucking his thumb and biting his lip,
But grasp it all, there may be more!
From the topless sky to the bottomless floor
With the heavy head and the fingertip:
All is not blind, obscene, and poor.
Socrates stands by me stockstill,
Teaching hope to my flickering will,
Pointing to the sky's inexorable blue
—Old Noumenon, come true, come true!

Where the sea gulls sleep or indeed where they fly
Is a place of different traffic. Although I
Consider the fishing bay (where I see them dip and curve
And purely glide) a place that weakens the nerve
Of will, and closes my eyes, as they should not be
(They should burn like the street-light all night quietly,
So that whatever is present will be known to me),
Nevertheless the gulls and the imagination
Of where they sleep, which comes to creation
In strict shape and color, from their dallying
Their wings slowly, and suddenly rallying
Over, up, down the arabesque of descent,
Is an old act enacted, my fabulous intent
When I skated, afraid of policemen, five years old,
In the winter sunset, sorrowful and cold,
Hardly attained to thought, but old enough to know
Such grace, so self-contained, was the best escape to know.

2

THE
REPETITIVE
HEART:
Poems
In Imitation of
The Fugue

All of us always turning away for solace

From the lonely room where the self must be honest,
All of us turning from being alone (at best
Boring) because what we want most is to be
Interested,
                play billiards, poking a ball
On the table, play baseball, batting a ball
On the diamond, play football, kicking a ball
On the gridiron,
                        seventy thousand applauding.

This amuses, this indeed is our solace:
Follow the bouncing ball! O, fellow, follow,
See what is here and clear, one thing repeated,
Bounding, evasive, caught and uncaught, fumbled
—Follow the bouncing ball; and thus you follow,
Fingering closely your breast on the left side,

The bouncing ball you turned from for solace.

Will You Perhaps Consent To Be

"méntre il vento, come fa, si tace"

Will you perhaps consent to be
Now that a little while is still
(Ruth of sweet wind) now that a little while
My mind's continuing and unreleasing wind
Touches this single of your flowers, this one only,
Will you perhaps consent to be
My many-branched, small and dearest tree?

My mind's continuing and unreleasing wind
—The wind which is wild and restless, tired and asleep,
The wind which is tired, wild and still continuing,
The wind which is chill, and warm, wet, soft, in every influence,
Lusts for Paris, Crete and Pergamus,
Is suddenly off for Paris and Chicago,
Judaea, San Francisco, the Midi
—May I perhaps return to you
Wet with an Attic dust and chill from Norway
My dear, so-many-branched smallest tree?

Would you perhaps consent to be
The very rack and crucifix of winter, winter's wild
Knife-edged, continuing and unreleasing,
Intent and stripping, ice-caressing wind?
My dear, most dear, so-many-branched tree
My mind's continuing and unreleasing wind
Touches this single of your flowers, faith in me,
Wide as the—sky!—accepting as the (air)!
—Consent, consent, consent to be
My many-branched, small and dearest tree.

All Clowns Are Masked and All Personae

All clowns are masked and all *personae*
Flow from choices; sad and gay, wise,
Moody and humorous are chosen faces,
And yet not so! For all are circumstances,
Given, like a tendency
To colds or like blond hair and wealth,
Or war and peace or gifts for mathematics,
Fall from the sky, rise from the ground, stick to us
In time, surround us: Socrates is mortal.

Gifts and choices! All men are masked,
And we are clowns who think to choose our faces
And we are taught in time of circumstances
And we have colds, blond hair and mathematics,
For we have gifts which interrupt our choices,
And all our choices grasp in Blind Man's Buff:
"My wife was very different, after marriage,"
"I practise law, but botany's my pleasure,"
Save postage stamps or photographs,
But save your soul! Only the past is immortal.

Decide to take a trip, read books of travel,
Go quickly! Even Socrates is mortal,
Mention the name of happiness: it is
Atlantis, Ultima Thule, or the limelight,
Cathay or Heaven. But go quickly
And remember: there are circumstances,
And he who chooses chooses what is given,
He who chooses is ignorant of Choice
—Choose love, for love is full of children,
Full of choices, children choosing
Botany, mathematics, law and love,
So full of choices! So full of children!
And the past is immortal, the future is inexhaustible!

Calmly we walk through this April's day,
Metropolitan poetry here and there,
In the park sit pauper and *rentier*,
The screaming children, the motor-car
Fugitive about us, running away,
Between the worker and the millionaire
Number provides all distances,
It is Nineteen Thirty-Seven now,
Many great dears are taken away,
What will become of you and me
(This is the school in which we learn . . .)
Besides the photo and the memory?
(. . . that time is the fire in which we burn.)

(This is the school in which we learn . . .)
What is the self amid this blaze?
What am I now that I was then
Which I shall suffer and act again,
The theodicy I wrote in my high school days
Restored all life from infancy,
The children shouting are bright as they run
(This is the school in which they learn . . .)
Ravished entirely in their passing play!
(. . . that time is the fire in which they burn.)

Avid its rush, that reeling blaze!
Where is my father and Eleanor?
Not where are they now, dead seven years,
But what they were then?
                    No more? No more?
From Nineteen-Fourteen to the present day,
Bert Spira and Rhoda consume, consume
Not where they are now (where are they now?)
But what they were then, both beautiful;

Each minute bursts in the burning room,
The great globe reels in the solar fire,
Spinning the trivial and unique away.
(How all things flash! How all things flare!)
What am I now that I was then?
May memory restore again and again
The smallest color of the smallest day:
Time is the school in which we learn,
Time is the fire in which we burn.

Dogs are Shakespearean, children are strangers.
Let Freud and Wordsworth discuss the child,
Angels and Platonists shall judge the dog,
The running dog, who paused, distending nostrils,
Then barked and wailed; the boy who pinched his sister,
The little girl who sang the song from *Twelfth Night*,
As if she understood the wind and rain,
The dog who moaned, hearing the violins in concert.
—O I am sad when I see dogs or children!
For they are strangers, they are Shakespearean.

Tell us, Freud, can it be that lovely children
Have merely ugly dreams of natural functions?
And you, too, Wordsworth, are children truly
Clouded with glory, learned in dark Nature?
The dog in humble inquiry along the ground,
The child who credits dreams and fears the dark,
Know more and less than you: they know full well
Nor dream nor childhood answer questions well:
You too are strangers, children are Shakespearean.

Regard the child, regard the animal,
Welcome strangers, but study daily things,
Knowing that heaven and hell surround us,
But this, this which we say before we're sorry,
This which we live behind our unseen faces,
Is neither dream, nor childhood, neither
Myth, nor landscape, final, nor finished,
For we are incomplete and know no future,
And we are howling or dancing out our souls
In beating syllables before the curtain:
We are Shakespearean, we are strangers.

Do the Others Speak of Me Mockingly, Maliciously?

"As in water face answereth to face, so the heart of man to man."

Do they whisper behind my back? Do they speak
Of my clumsiness? Do they laugh at me,
Mimicking my gestures, retailing my shame?
I'll whirl about, denounce them, saying
That they are shameless, they are treacherous,
No more my friends, nor will I once again
Never, amid a thousand meetings in the street,
Recognize their faces, take their hands,
Not for our common love or old times' sake:
They whispered behind my back, they mimicked me.

I know the reason why, I too have done this,
Cruel for wit's sake, behind my dear friend's back,
And to amuse betrayed his private love,
His nervous shame, her habit, and their weaknesses;
I have mimicked them, I have been treacherous,
For wit's sake, to amuse, because their being weighed
Too grossly for a time, to be superior,
To flatter the listeners by this, the intimate,
Betraying the intimate, but for the intimate,
To free myself of friendship's necessity,
Fearing from time to time that they would hear,
Denounce me and reject me, say once for all
That they would never meet me, take my hands,
Speaking for old times' sake and our common love.

What an unheard-of thing it is, in fine,
To love another and equally be loved!
What sadness and what joy! How cruel it is
That pride and wit distort the heart of man,
How vain, how sad, what cruelty, what need,

For this is true and sad, that I need them
And they need me. What can we do? We need
Each other's clumsiness, each other's wit,
Each other's company and our own pride. I need
My face unshamed, I need my wit, I cannot
Turn away. We know our clumsiness,
Our weakness, our necessities, we cannot
Forget our pride, our faces, our common love.

I Am to My Own Heart Merely a Serf

I am to my own heart merely a serf
And follow humbly as it glides with autos
And come attentive when it is too sick,
In the bad cold of sorrow much too weak,
To drink some coffee, light a cigarette
And think of summer beaches, blue and gay.
I climb the sides of buildings just to get
Merely a gob of gum, all that is left
Of its infatuation of last year.
Being the servant of incredible assumption,
Being to my own heart merely a serf.

I have been sick of its cruel rule, as sick
As one is sick of chewing gum all day;
Only inside of sleep did all my anger
Spend itself, restore me to my role,
Comfort me, bring me to the morning
Willing and smiling, ready to be of service,
To box its shadows, lead its brutish dogs,
Knowing its vanity the vanity of waves.

But when sleep too is crowded, when sleep too
Is full of chores impossible and heavy,
The looking for white doors whose numbers are
Different and equal, that is, infinite,
The carriage of my father on my back,
Last summer, 1910, and my own people,
The government of love's great polity,
The choice of taxes, the production
Of clocks, of lights, and horses, the location
Of monuments, of hotels and of rhyme,
Then, then, in final anger, I wake up!
Merely wake up once more,
                  once more to resume

The unfed hope, the unfed animal,
Being the servant of incredible assumption,
Being to my own heart merely a serf.

Abraham and Orpheus, Be With Me Now

Abraham and Orpheus, be with me now:
You saw your love's face abstract, the weak-kneed stilts,
You saw and knew, and knew how near "no more"
(As one who scrutinizes mystery, the air),
How poised on nothing, weighted on the air,
The touched, seen substance, the substance of care:
Surround me, be round me, be with me like the air,
Abraham and Orpheus, be with me now.

Love love exhausts and time goes round and round,
Time circles in its idiot defeat,
And that which circles falls, falls endlessly,
Falls endlessly, no music shapes the air
Which did, can, shall restore the end of care,
For love exhausts itself and time goes round,
I shudder in the traffic, buildings stand,
Will fall and night will fall, the electric light be snapped
To spread its yellow genius on the floor,
And you knew too who knew and knew "no more"
That love exhausts itself and falls and time goes round.

Abraham and Orpheus, be with me now:
No longer the grandstand, nor the balcony,
Nor the formal window gives me cool perspective:
Love sucked me to the moving street below,
I see the price of care, turning to keep,
I am a price, I turn to keep, I care,
But time which circles dissipates all care,
As you knew too, who lifted up the knife,
And you, musician in the after-life,
Drowning in the shadow all love always bears,
As every solid thing must shadow in the light:
I ask your learned presence, I care and fear,
Abraham and Orpheus, be near, be near.

The Heavy Bear Who Goes With Me

"the withness of the body"

The heavy bear who goes with me,
A manifold honey to smear his face,
Clumsy and lumbering here and there,
The central ton of every place,
The hungry beating brutish one
In love with candy, anger, and sleep,
Crazy factotum, dishevelling all,
Climbs the building, kicks the football,
Boxes his brother in the hate-ridden city.

Breathing at my side, that heavy animal,
That heavy bear who sleeps with me,
Howls in his sleep for a world of sugar,
A sweetness intimate as the water's clasp,
Howls in his sleep because the tight-rope
Trembles and shows the darkness beneath.
—The strutting show-off is terrified,
Dressed in his dress-suit, bulging his pants,
Trembles to think that his quivering meat
Must finally wince to nothing at all.

That inescapable animal walks with me,
Has followed me since the black womb held,
Moves where I move, distorting my gesture,
A caricature, a swollen shadow,
A stupid clown of the spirit's motive,
Perplexes and affronts with his own darkness,
The secret life of belly and bone,
Opaque, too near, my private, yet unknown,
Stretches to embrace the very dear
With whom I would walk without him near,
Touches her grossly, although a word

Would bare my heart and make me clear,
Stumbles, flounders, and strives to be fed
Dragging me with him in his mouthing care,
Amid the hundred million of his kind,
The scrimmage of appetite everywhere.

A dog named Ego, the snowflakes as kisses
Fluttered, ran, came with me in December,
Snuffing the chill air, changing, and halting,
There where I walked toward seven o'clock,
Sniffed at some interests hidden and open,
Whirled, descending, and stood still, attentive
Seeking their peace, the stranger, unknown,
With me, near me, kissed me, touched my wound,
My simple face, obsessed and pleasure bound.

"Not free, no liberty, rock that you carry,"
So spoke Ego in his cracked and harsh voice,
While snowflakes kissed me and satisfied minutes,
Falling from some place half believed and unknown,
"You will not be free, nor ever alone,"
So spoke Ego, "Mine is the kingdom,
Dynasty's bone: you will not be free,
Go, choose, run, you will not be alone."

"Come, come, come," sang the whirling snowflakes,
Evading the dog who barked at their smallness,
"Come!" sang the snowflakes, "Come here! and here!"
How soon at the sidewalk, melted, and done,
One kissed me, two kissed me! So many died!
While Ego barked at them, swallowed their touch,
Ran this way! And that way! While they slipped to the ground,
Leading him further and farther away,
While night collapsed amid the falling,
And left me no recourse, far from my home,
And left me no recourse, far from my home.

Time's Dedication

My heart beating, my blood running,
The light brimming,
My mind moving, the ground turning,
My eyes blinking, the air flowing,
The clock's quick-ticking,
Time moving, time dying,
Time perpetually perishing!
Time is farewell! Time is farewell!

Abide with me: do not go away,
But not as the dead who do not walk,
And not as the statue in the park,
And not as the rock which meets the wave,
But quit the dance from which is flowing
Wishes and turns, gestures and voices,
Angry desire and fallen tomorrow,
Quit the dance from which is flowing
Your blood and beauty: stand still with me.

We cannot stand still: time is dying,
We are dying: Time is farewell!

Stay then, stay! Wait now for me,
Deliberately, with care and circumspection,
Deliberately
Stop.
When we are in step, running together,
Our pace equal, our motion one,
Then we will be well, parallel and equal,
Running together down the macadam road,
Walking together,
Controlling our pace before we get old,
Walking together on the receding road,
Like Chaplin and his orphan sister,
Moving together through time to all good.

3

CORIOLANUS

AND

HIS MOTHER

A Dream

of

Knowledge

Act One:
"O Me! Make You a Sword of Me!"

Theatre, the place to stare, rustle of programs,
Many have come, are being seated. The house
Is full, the audience is distinguished,
And in a box-seat sit five ghosts, and one,
A boy with muffled voice full of emotion.
The lights dim, half-darkness now accents
The footlights' glitter before the curtain. The curtain
Rises on the heart of man,
      Rome, Rome,
The history-ridden arena shown by
A temple painted on a canvas backdrop;
On fluted columns, fat and white, there rests
The pediment wherein a writhing frieze
Of armed men strain to kill the other team
World without end, world without end of hatred.

The rumor of a crowd comes near. Many
Come crowding on the stage, bunched in their anger,
Holding aloft their clubs, their staves, their torches,
Knowing a mob's emotion.
      Hunger, debts,
Poverty bring this demonstration. One,
Brutus, articulate, using their interest,
Mounts near the temple, tells them what they mean:

"Two years ago, you poor people one day
Gathered together; one encouraging another,
You all forsook the city, stood upon
A height beside the Tiber, made no show
Of actual rebellion, except to cry,
As you marched up and down the meager height:
'The rich men drive us from the city. The rich men
Leave us no air, no water, nor even ground
To bury our dead. To live in Rome, to live

In this great city is to be used and slain
In the murderous war warred to increase
The rich man's riches.'
                    So! So!
You cried then, you poor people, so you were given
What?
The usual concessions which, as usual,
Made you forget the reason for your pain.
But hunger you cannot forget! Awake!
Seize your enemy, O, grasp his throat,
Demand your right to live, your right to eat,
Have you no right to eat? He who denies it
Murders you! Deny the rich! Deny
Your murderers! Shout in their perfumed ears
That you refuse to die while they are rich!"

Their roar responds. He pants, the actor's pause,
To show the large emotion on his face.

—And now, shuffling, diverting gaze,
Toga'd Menenius, canny patrician, comes,
Fat and untidy, dragging his robe along,
Good-humored extravert, rosy and robust,
And not too finicky:
                    "Listen!" he says,
Contemptuous yet soothing, knowing their will
And their necessity; divided from them
And so against them; requiring them
And therefore politic; consoling them
With the old Platonic metaphor in which
The state, that knot of common weakness,
Consistent need, poor fear, and aching will,
Becomes an animal or organism
Wherein each organ must deny itself
That the great corpse may be well-fed.
"How metaphors may serve the ruling class,
Hypostasis itself shall soothe the poor!"
Sighs one great ghost beside me, as I stare,

Knowing not where I am but everywhere,
Lavish of mind and in attention such
Each whisper thunders in the crowded air,
Striking the heart where all the meanings touch,
All pieties, all choices, every care!

"Listen," Menenius says. "Be sensible,
We do our best to handle everything,
Be patient, boys, and in the end, you know,
Everyone will be satisfied."
                                    But now
Marcius comes striding through the burly crowd,
O like an obelisk his obvious posture,
His look as Caesar's face strict on a coin,
Barbarous strength and beauty there:

"You stink!" he cries. "You scum!" he shouts, shocked by
Their protest, offended by their being,
Nursing in mind, older than any thought,
A hatred of all who issue sweat, urine,
Or excrement, the child's profound distaste
Once for all smitten, never, alas! outworn.

"So you assume our role, faeces of man!
The garrulity of your idleness
Swelling your vast conceit, you arrogant
Presumptuous intolerable apes!
If the nobility would merely once
Abate their maudlin rule, I, all alone,
I, I, I,
Would thrash a hundred thousand of your kind!"
Bullying empty extravagance, his tongue
Betrays a pathic source beneath the eye,
The wound and rage not of a ruling class
(Whose prudent tact Menenius displayed,
Joking and friendly) but himself alone
Is represented in his gross excess,
Himself alone prepossessed long ago

By an antipathy un-understood,
A tenderness moving the mind unknown.

"O don't mind us, we only work here and
And, hunger breaks stone walls, and, dogs must eat,
And, meat is made for mouths. Does God provide
Grain for the rich men only?"
                                        So Brutus stammered,
Stricken and awed by his loud prejudice:
"O now you are their tongue!" Marcius replied,
"I must consult your heart before I blink,
You, paid official, who, on their discontent
Erect your dignity——"
                                        A sudden cry,
A newsboy loudly shouting "War!
War is declared! The Volscians are in arms!"
Quickly the meeting is transformed,
Marcius forgets his enemy,
The bitter broken poor forget their need,
And all adjourn, each one to find his role,
In the lightning's dramatic thrust and sequent moan.

"So by death's poverty is poverty escaped,
Negation negated in the chess of death,"
Says the great ghost beside me in the box,
While murmurs move the darkened audience,
"War being the state's good health, the state, alas!
Being, as knock-kneed Hegel said,
Organized pain, a formal agony:
In war's magnified ache, brilliantly blared,
The poor mistake their grandeur and their grief;
Adding their weakness, they affirm the state,
The stranger's grain, the stranger's wealth is seized!
The ruling class in intuition know
That thus the state persists, and thus,
By the extension of their perpetual need
Unto another's property, they are maintained,
And by the expense of anger on the stranger,

The poor are fed."
                  So, as the curtain falls
Upon the risen interest of all,
Marx bites his nails, resumes his revery,
Ghosts being possessed by consciousness,
Consumed by memory, and powerless.

A new scene. On a side street. Twilight
Blackens the roof-tops. Brutus and his fellow,
The voices of the poor, confer in whispers,
Hold in analysis the soul of Marcius,
Surd irreducible, a glittering diamond,
Unpurchased by their tactic or their smile,
Occult to them.
             "Listen! Speak quietly.
Was ever man so proud as is this Marcius?"
"No man so proud,
              he has no equal, none."
"When we were made their voices did you see
How his lip formed a sneer direct at me?"
"He mocks the moon, he holds in his contempt
The shadow which he treads at noon."
                     "And God himself
Is mocked, I think, in this man's singular heart."
"He is insane, alone in his fantasy,
Gazing at his sole image in a glass
Where no light shines but arbitrary pride."
"We are not safe until he's cast aside."

Another scene: it is the sitting room
Where wife and mother of the hero sew
To beguile attention while their hearts await
News of the war, the distant thunder's boom.

"Sing merrily, enjoy this strong today,"
So says the Roman mother, the widowed one,
Moved by her own obsession,
                 "Daughter, sing,

Were he my husband as he is my son,
This would delight me O much more than when
In the ecstasy of the darkness I conceived,
Moved by the thrusting self-delighting spoon
Which made my son, my spear."

                  So she exults
That there is war and that her son makes war,
And with an urgent dogma she insists
That the meek girl, his wife, shall also feel
Her own harsh appetite,
                while Sigmund Freud
Mutters beside me in the haunted night,
"This is the origin, this, this is the place,
Mother in love with son and son with her,
And his aloneness in the womb began,
Always unhappy apart from that tight cache:
O womb and egg, nervous environment,
How you have marred and marked this childhood's man!
Unconscionable bag which none evade,
How your great warmth commits him to the shade."

"O no!" The black-browed ghost in haste replies,
As the curtain falls, and furniture is moved,
And the orchestra tunes up, the hidden musician
Tightening and pricking his violin in the pit,
"But as a drowning man must cherish land,
And as in hunger bread must be soft gold,
So, in a society which lives by war,
The soldier boy is best. As the assassin
Admires the knife, as the mariner
Considers the sea, as the tailor
Respects the wish to dress, O as
The leaning doctor listens for the heart,
Man murders, travels, sews and bends in fear
To get the good which the means of life make dear!
Man lives and dies to buy the dears of life,
Every man dies for that which gives him life!
Not that poor widow, but society

86

Nursed him to being, taught him what to be:
She is the actual mother, only for her
Has he become the narrow murderer!"

At which the curtain rises, silencing him:

Distant, we see Corioli's great fort,
We hear the shocking guns, the thud and flash;
A team in miniature is running forth
In loose array, as if involved in games,
And as two football teams in scrimmage there
Men mix and wrestle, grunt, leap forward, fall,
The rush, the furor, pop! bang! whoa!
All shows in little to our frigid gaze.
The cry, the anger, the chaos, and the gong
Are far too distant to be serious.
The trumpet's imagination and éclat
Are much too large for each one striving there,
Aware of running men and puffs of smoke
And prickly sweat and nothing else but fear.
The while, to our perspective, nothing near,
The moving pins lack actuality,
Until a messenger comes breathlessly,
Speaks through a megaphone the victory:

"Marcius! Marcius defeats the defensive host,
Marcius alone! While we hung back, afraid,
And angered him until he called us swine,
Timid cows, geese, not men, he walked ahead
Unto the Volscians' ranks, who, being amazed,
Retreat, enter their gates, begin to run,
Marcius upon them,

             while we keep safely back,
An obvious danger there, he follows them
Into the gates, which they raise up! And thus
He's trapped! Alone within the gates! Himself
Alone to answer all the city!

            'Slain!

Slain doubtless,' says our general,
While all, knowing him, know his iron and rage,
Bow heads and feel, though namelessly, in awe
That there, his enemies on every side,
Occurs his apotheosis before he dies,
His marrow satisfaction,
                              until he runs
Phenomenal! miraculous! Upon our epitaphs
Out from the gates, waving his glossy sword,
Having somehow beaten all men from him,
Opened the gates and issued thence
                              to cry,
'Again! And more! Renew the attack once more!'
(Although the subtle blood streams from his limbs)
And curses us as pusillanimous,
Naming us wooden things, things dull, clogged,
Inanimate,
                   and cries, obsessed, 'Once more!
Attack once more!' As if, with pathic hate,
Misanthropos with sensuous emotion,
Hating all men, he was fulfilled in war.

Lartius our general demurs and then permits
Marcius to attack once more, with volunteers,
Who, when with famous bravado he calls on them,
Painting with fustian voice the life-in-death,
Offer their wills to him, shout, cheering him,
Take him upon their shoulders, at which he cries,
Narcissus baritone in brittle armor:
'O me alone! Make you a sword of me!'

Elsewhere Cominius, a normal one,
Admits retreat, calls foolish further war,
Considers true and Roman a pause *pro tem,*
Knowing not Marcius' walking dream,
                              who now
Leads the attack, seeks out of all men, one,
His utmost foe, Aufidius (for hate,

Love, and desire concentrate their blaze),
Their bravest man, known to him long before.

And the attack succeeds, the Volscians flee,
Aufidius is met, but in the vicious strife,
Then, striking each other with his being's whip,
Each grasping his self as individual,
Aufidius is rescued by his men,
Even as the fortress falls,
                    Marcius the winner,
Marcius victorious, Caius Marcius hero!
His obsessed radical spirit ruling the day."

The megaphoned one retires. Now we see
All met to formalize the victory:

Cominius wishes to render him
The glittering glory of the circumstance
And in ovation rounds such speech for him
As must delight all sensible of fame,
Fame the huge face confronting every man
Who walks amid his fellows, finding in them
The audience of his play and satisfaction.
"—No man may live alone, but with his mother
Having lived once, he's brutally bereft
By every absence, every solitude——"
So interrupts a great ghost by my side,
Private of all for whom truth is a bride!

But Marcius is dismayed, shy as young men,
Or prudery of those whose intense sex
Denies itself.
                His secret vice thus published
Amid the torchlight scene, the dress parade,
Enormously gratified and therefore shamed
(As two tugging their love become aware
That a whole public laugh, enjoy and stare),
Blushes, feigns modesty.

And then, when Lartius
Gives him ten times his proper share of all
Won on the field, he must refuse at once,
Money's not relevant unto his measure,
And the refusal may dress his nakedness,
His sheer delight, his shame to be delighted
—*His* sort of heart to depend on another one!

The rank and file misunderstand him. This,
They think, is courtesy to them.
                              They cheer as if
Marcius bequeathed them immortality!

But their applause strikes instantly
Hemorrhage of anger from him. That *he*, Marcius,
Should seek their plaudits, look to them!
—Flies from his tongue the phlegm and spit of rage:
No one may touch him, none; no one reward him,
Pay him. His self must be self-fed. He is
His own, not theirs.
                    Cominius suggests
That this excess is sentimental
(The rest stand by, perplexed), but chooses then
(Of subtle intuition *le mot juste*)
The one garland this shaven virgin will wear,
A name, a name additional and new
(Not to exclude his own but fatten it),
New word, new syllable, new tone for his
Intense selfhood to breathe and whisper:
CAIUS MARCIUS CORIOLANUS,
                              Marcius,
Blushing and moved, consents and turns away.
"His autograph, his signature, his own,
As in Napoleon, Alcibiades,
Jacob whose name was Israel, and Saul,
Translated at Damascus, Caesar, Czar,
Kaiser, and Charlemagne, George Eliot,
Stella, Vanessa, Aloysius, Jones,

Between the anonymous and nomenclature
Both vaudeville and history resume
The continuum of fame and mockery
In which all wince and which is poetry!"
—Thus mocks one ghost who gazes there beside me.

The curtain falls. The orchestra begins,
Bomb! Bomb! Bomb! Beethoven sobs.
He too beside me in the crowded box,
And slumped in his cliché, chin to his breast:
Bomb! Bomb! Bomb! What awe and care!
Then sweetly, thinly, fluted the melody
Of the soul in private pitying itself,
Tenderly touching every grouch and sore.

—And then the music ceases. The bright lights flood
Theatre, audience, our straining gaze, and now,
Amazed as never before, myself I see
Enter between the curtains' folds, appear
As many titter and some clap hands in glee,
A sad young clown in gown of domino,
X-ray, cartoon, Picasso's freak in blue,
From the box-seat I see myself on show.

I come, I said, to be useful and to entertain. What else can one do? Between the acts something must be done to occupy our minds or we become too aware of our great emptiness. It is true, we might converse with one another. But then we would learn again how little all of us have to say to each other. Love is not American. Neither is conversation, but that is not exactly what I mean.

One ought to be amusing, but unfortunately I know very few witty sayings, entertaining stories. I find that my idea of the comical is not, as they say, objective. I have tried for some time to invent a good story for this occasion, but the best I could do is this new wrinkle, entitled "Turning the Tables": ABC says to DEF: "Who was that lady I saw you with last night? Some fun, hey, boy!" DEF, offended by the lightness with which his passion is regarded, replies: "That was no lady, that was *your* wife." A good story too, at least to me, is Stendhal's remark on first eating ice cream: "What a pity it is not a sin!" Becoming more serious in order to approach nearer to my true subject, I recall the fact that Fichte drank champagne for the first time when his infant boy said "I" for the first time. Let me continue with two more quotations bearing on this Laocoön-like process and presentation which we are here to see. "I can hire half the working class to fight the other half." So said Jay Gould at about the same time that Engels, intimate friend of a member of the audience, was observing with the most perfect justice that the most appalling evil produced by class conflict was its corruption and degradation of the *ruling class*—barbarism, inexorable cynicism, contempt for all values on the part of those who enjoy the greatest benefits of society. Sophocles observes that man is the most admirable of beings. It is true. The most disgusting also, one ought to add. It is dialectical. The possibility of the one means the possibility of the other.

Now take this world's champion of men, Coriolanus, whose life we passively suffer to step over our faces (as we sit here, in the prepared darkness). All things are tied together, though sometimes loosely. Hence, more and more facts are dragged on the stage, as this moving individual passes before the footlights. Who knows if there will, indeed, be sufficient room? No doubt that I am an intruder, but try to eject me. The sky cannot be excluded. It is the greatest natural object. The state cannot be omitted. It is the greatest artificial object. The individual requires our focused gaze. He is the greatest subject, natural and artificial. Then there is his mother, his wife, his child, all his fathers, all his children. What an enormous crowd it may become! And the audience is already so complex, so full of foreigners.

Besides, there are questions of emphasis. "The individual is the only verifiable actuality, the individual, his experience from moment to moment." So said one in French at about the same time as Lev Davidovich, better known as Trotzky, justly remarked that "The individual—is an abstraction!" He is right and yet you know and so do I as we sit here in this theatre—the essential stareotorium, one might say—we both know that we cannot regard the warm identity beneath our faces as being no more than an abstraction. Man is always *in* the world, yes! inconceivable apart from being surrounded by a greater whole than himself. And yet he is at the same time himself and in and by himself and by traveling here and there may separate himself from any particular interior in which he finds himself. There is a thought which will take a considerable amount of chewing and then you will only have to spit it out again. As I said, all this bears upon what is taking place here. Also on Coriolanus the individual. Food, for example, improves the spirit, coffee consoles the soul. Most men, to quote again, lead lives of quiet desperation, the victims, all of them, of innumerable intentions. Hence the enormous *spiritual* and emotional quality of food and drink. There is also tobacco and alcohol, although wine too is not American.

Why be desperate, even quietly? Thus one might ask. Because one end merely leads to another one, one activity to another one, one activity to another in an inexhaustible *endlessnessness* which is exasperating, metaphysically speaking, although such speech is not the fashion. Do not, however, be disconsolate nor given over to unutterable despair. Consider the nature of pleasure. It is a maligned word, meaning merely the innocence and intrinsicality of being, each thing and each state taken as final and for itself. A cup of coffee destroys your sadness. To be born, we are told, is the greatest of all pains—all else a dilution and weakening which offends the masochist. Though this be but a gynecologist's truth, yet let us remember it. Pleasure is what it is as is the rose. It justifies itself. To have pleasure, to be pleased, to enjoy oneself, that is sufficient, and only the Philistine asks: What for? Although there is a question of the permanent, the intermittent, the conflicting, and the exclusive, but let us not discuss this now.

Pleasure has a hundred thousand obvious forms, plentiful variety for the most fickle spirit. Pleasure of convalescence (how voluptuous weakness can be); pleasure of need (a dry crust of bread); pleasure of the first time and the last time; pleasure of mere looking (as the sunlight delights itself upon the tumbling fountain, as the small morning makes the metropolis unreal); pleasure of being a child (mixture of curiosity, wantonness, and the gradual stages); pleasure of having a child (O my son Absalom, graduating from high school!); pleasure of discovery and pleasure of memory, freshness and nostalgic sweetness, surprise and return. Pleasure of arising, the keenness of breakfast; pleasure of sleeping (there one is Caesar); the pleasure of the old, a stronger tobacco, to possess the time that is past; the pleasure of the young, who are not yet tired; the pleasure of marriage—the mystery of being called Mrs. for the first time; the pleasure, do not deny it, of the funeral (that, after all, the conclusion should have a certain sublimity and repose); pleasure of the grandchild (a difficult pleasure, needing so much strength to last that long and so many refusals, year after year); the pleasure of ritual, the gloves drawn on precisely; the pleasure of spontaneity, kissed by the overjoyed, the wave's foaming white head, touched at the lips.

Delight in the silver, delight in the rock, delight in the soft silk, delight in the stubble, delight in the thimble, delight in the mountain, happiness of the virgin, the satisfaction of custom, joy in denial (the firmness of the soldier, the rigor of the surgeon, the formal athlete, the painstaking scholar), and the sweetness of saying yes.

Eating too is a fine thing, though it makes difficulties (do not laugh; economy and original sin may in fact be inseparable): and there is the pleasure at the conclusion of effort, the best of all delights, as the swimmer returned to the sunlight, his being glowing in the warmth responsive to the shocking chill of the waters (surrounded by them, he understood his body). Or the pleasure of the idle who, prone, full-length, made almost unknowingly a few exact perceptions, especially of those who hurry. And the satisfaction of the guilty (thus to have an identity not dissipated by their weakness); the delight of the famous, their self-regard coming from the outside; the joy of narration, thus to invent and, inventing, understand; the sweetness of the musician, from thunder and whisper tone's moving constellations; and also the pleasure of small pains, the sweetness of anger, as Homer observes; the delight of the game (from out of the scrimmage came the tall and plunging figure and ran to a touchdown!); the pleasure of the task, the pleasure of the opus (the span, the parts, the detail, the conclusion); the delight, clear as fresh water, of theory and knowing (O lucid mathematics!) To each age and each stage a special quality of satisfaction, enough for everyone, and enough for all time, no need to compete. States of being suffice. Let the handsome be familiar with the looking-glass, and let the ugly be gourmets (since so many cannot be beautiful, let eating be socially superior to portraits). Let this unwarranted sadness come to an end, sound and fury signify a multitude of enjoyments, the pleasure of pain, the pleasure indeed of pleasure. Pleasure believes in friends, pleasure creates communities, pleasure crumbles faces into smiles, pleasure links hand in hand, pleasure restores, pain is the most selfish thing. And yet, I know, all this is nothing, nothing consoles one, and our problem and pain are still before us.

Let us continue to gaze upon it. Let us, I say, make a few sharp clear definite observations before we die. Let us judge all things according to the measure of our hearts (otherwise we cannot live). Let us require of ourselves the strength and power to view our selves and the heart of man *with* disgust.

Act Two:
"His Soaring Insolence, the Common Muck"

Absurd and precarious my presence there,
Looped by the spotlight in assured discourse,
Harangue, imperative, prayer and wish,
True story and confession, who knows what?
Double, absorbed, monstrous, amazed, ashamed,
With much relief myself I see retire
And as the curtain rises on ACT TWO
Regain my sense of place, sharpened anew.

Triumphal march, the formidable Arch,
Thick crowds, harassed police, the brilliant sunlight.
—Bearing the truck of all his honors, wearing
The hat of his new name,
                         puffed by the herald,
Hailed by the populace, Marcius returns,
Aquiline profile, statuesque in the car.

Some who await him stand in attitudes
Equivocal; for perspectivity
Possesses infinite degrees,
Every nuance of love and hate therein,
As if all were a metaphor of place, profound,
Elliptic, solid, flat, far, thin and round!

The ruling class, as in Menenius,
Take simple pride in their validity
Displayed in him. The tribunes fear in him
Pure tyranny. His mother
Hopes he has many wounds, exults, exults,
Mouths of the death which he bestows as if
She would have all restored to the dark womb.

Cannons burst! Sirens scream! The crowd
Enjoys its own excitement. The occasion
Engenders its own increase, applause

96

Engenders applause, whirling confetti,
Roses and laurel fall,
                    all gaze, stare, cheer,
Murmur of him. Nurse holds up baby boy
As gaze may be infectious, cook is dressed
In Sunday's clothes, the old, the strange, the ill
Who stay in private rooms the whole year long,
Press against rich and poor, packed at the curb,
Passionate to see him, hardly aware
Of the tumult, the brass, the flashing heat,
Their congregated act,
                    while Marcius stands
Hiding his strange emotion amid the roar,
Secretly pleased despite himself, ashamed
To take of their plaudits so much flushing pleasure,
Guilty to think he gets his joy from them,
And half-aware of their powerful entity.
"*Noli me tangere!* How large they shout,
Each would partake of my world's championship,
Each thinks himself myself and I am fucked
By every craven knight vicarious there.
—Yet what a sweetness is that roaring kiss
Spreading in waves throughout the whorish air."

Arrived to the station where his mother waits,
Also his wife, his child, his friends,
Rapt self-absorption fades or rather descends
Unto that great primordial circumstance
Which holds him yet.
                    "O Mother, Mother," kneeling,
Thus he descends to her. "All that I did
I did for you."
                    The snub-nosed Freud exclaims,
Seated beside me in the heavy box,
"This is the place! Early historians
Call this Volumnia his wife. Avon alone
Grasps the identity of mother and bride,
The infant's choice, whatever man decide!"

His wife waits silently, ungreeted by him,
Wholly unseen,
                till mother reminds the boy
His son's meek mother waits to be recognized,
Speaks with slight irony of his new name,
Strictly retains the womb's authority.

Quick change: the Capitol: the Senate's chamber,
The ruling class resolved to raise him up
Highest in office and complete in power,
All public hope fulfilled.
                Cominius
Addresses the Senate, recites his life *in toto*
—He's interrupted as our squeamish virgin
Arises, tortured, will not stay, he says,
To hear his nothings monstered, he a monster
Thus to respond, monstrously delicate,
And make his exit like a puking girl
Upset by joy.
                Cominius continues,
Utters the public face which all can see,
The abstract terms of all biography,
Hiding desire and shame, the personal one
Known to himself in the bedroom all alone.
And yet the bragged *données* contain his soul,
His self *pur sang,* if but their rule be seen
—Marcius, at sixteen, a mere boy still,
The most precocious soldier! Again and again
War after war, the champion in each,
Until before Corioli his war alone,
Sole, single, absolute, *per se,* alone
(Aseity such as is God's alone)
Against the enemy despite his wounds
Until their vast defeat.
                Cominius
Proposes him Consul as his meager due——

"Why," says the ghost next to the unknown one

(The small anonymous fifth whose face is hidden
By a white mask un-understood by all,
And who calls up in me an unknown fear),
"Why does his lauding advocate omit
His irreparable childhood, infancy
And foetusdom, the animal
Delighted by the breast, the boy denied
A role in the running game, the boy's amaze
When he walked home alone from school,
                                                                    enjoyed
His revery, found solitude most sweet,
Prided himself thereon, and felt contempt
For all not self-contained as he,
                                                the boy,
He who would skate alone on the hard lake
Under the faery moon, Diana's day,
The child, the foetus too, the widow's son,
Her only son, who fed him, praised him, warned
Her dainty son to keep from common boys,
Showed herself gratified in him alone:
The past is always present, present as past,
It grasps us like Athena by the hair!"

"By six," the father of Nicomachus
Murmurs to me, "By six, the man is made,
Habitus, virtue, and his lasting shade."
"Before his birth," the later ghost replies,
"His greatest mother chose his greatest prize!"
"The past is always present, present as past,
It grasps us like Athena by the hair,
The hair above the mind whose thick coils knot
Until the soul arises from the body's rot."
So said the saddest ghost beside me there.

The whole Senate consents, unhesitant,
Calls Marcius back, confirms him Consul if,
A mere formality, the poor people give
Their votes to him, when, as the custom is,

99

He stands before them dressed in ashen gown,
Showing his wounds to them.
                              Marcius, nauseous once more,
Asks the omission of this ritual,
Asks that the right be taken from the people,
Maintains the bad smell of the people's breath,
Calls this a braggart nakedness and shame
—But the tribunes insist.
                              Outside, the people
Discuss their Marcius, laugh, admire him,
Holding themselves in humorous contempt,
Feigning each other's stupidity, till one,
Amid their serious, mock-serious
Discussion of their power and his virtue
And his contempt of them and yet his due,
States that all this is well and good, but he
Must take a leak.
                    "Little the people wish,"
Says one great ghost in that distinguished box,
"Little they get. Being nor good nor evil,
Except as driven, they desire merely
A bit of salt for cucumbers in May,
A movie once a week, a game to play,
A visit to the zoo, two weeks in June,
Someone with whom to speak, something
To read while eating, someone to touch
Wholly and privately, both hard and soft,
A little self-respect, a place to sleep,
Stories of immortality.
                          Their whole wish is
Modest and not too urgent till the strict
Inevitable mathematic come to reduce
Little to nothing, almost nothing, a crust,
That some may get still more and more,
                                        they must!"
Shuddering as a young girl does
Examined by doctors with mustachios,
Our Marcius, standing in a little box,

Appears before the people.
                              Crouching rabbits
Regard the square-jawed lion, who is dressed
In his own nakedness and in
Humility's gray gown. He asks their votes
Precisely as he would and as he must,
The bluster voice which always hides the shy
Betraying his self-infatuated I:
"My own desert requires no less! Keep clean
Your teeth and wash your faces! Voices!
I sweated for your voices, for your voices
I tore my heart in fury!
                              O I never
Desired to trouble the poor by begging from them!"

"You never loved the common people,"
                              one
Meekly and hopefully asserts
—"Honor me then, dear Sirs, my virtue is
Not to be common in my love. Your voices!
Your voices, Gentlemen!"
                              His irony
Tortures himself and merely, so it seems,
Perplexes the mild and generous poor people
Passing before him in his little box.
—Gladly they recognize his wounds, his virtues,
Freely they choose him, grant him their full voices,
Strive with his mocking words, mean well, depart
Aware of something wrong somewhat somewhere,
With him, with them, with both, who knows, who knows?

Indeed who knows?
                              Cupid, a nearby fountain,
Pisses his puddle on the Square, chipped boy
Piercing our hero's to-fro heart.
                              Beside me
Stagira murmurs approval of the scene
—"Avon, a mother's son, knew what men mean,

A pencil of all hearts."
                    The later ghost
Marvels to see one man detest the host,
Speaks of the secret and gigantic mother
Which makes each man a sister and a brother.
The orchestra tunes up: a spreading moan
—Ludwig van Beethoven, Marcius in tone,
Rumors in woodwinds all that is to come,
Massing crescendo of the poor king numb.

Meanwhile we see the tribunes huddle,
Winking, conspiratorial, malicious,
Come to the people with their facile tongues
And in contempt of them much more confirmed,
Equipped and cynical than Marcius is,
Quickly persuade the people to reverse
The election, take away his crown, reject him,
Till with their cheap ken they transform the people
Into an ignorant passionate crowd,
Willed to the hurt of our undrowned Narcissus,
Our self-regardant lion, his raided heart.

"Who is the fifth ghost in this heavy box?
Who is the small masked one who says no word?
Tell me his name!"
                    But no one answers me.
"O tell me, tell me, O Immanuel Kant,"
I said when they were silent, frenzied then,
"You who diminished knowledge, inverted hope,
Divided day from night, assigned the night
The avid dreams of the practical heart."

JUSTICE

What! The same voluble fellow again—such is your speech with your-self, I suppose, upon seeing me again, though this time in a dress suit with a top hat (as if to appeal to the snob and fop in every man, or at least to the upper-class sentiments in all of the lower and middle class). Yes! What a buttonholing mariner! What a jack-in-the-box I am, but truly with a decent motive—to entertain, to be useful—and also to arrive at a point. What point? I do not actually know, except that there must be a point and when I get there I will recognize it, though I scarcely expect to get there very soon, and one who did would equal all the seven wonders of nature of the ancients—the camel, the rainbow, the echo, the cuckoo, the Negro, the volcano, and the sirocco.

I have been thinking about justice. Naturally: look at what surrounds us. Justice: a fine word and immediately suggesting how beautiful a thing the fact must be, if there is such a fact, either possible or actual. A round, complete, self-contained datum, like an enormous globe radiating a dazzling light which illuminates every corner, subterfuge, and mystery *between* human beings, not creating, as the sun does (being like all natural things involved in the dialectic of nature) so many morbid shadows, and the black broom of night at once with the bright bloom of day.

What could I think of, desiring to amuse as well as instruct, also to be pleased and to learn myself—of what but the ancient short story made known to me in childhood by my crippled father, a brief history which has prepossessed me to this day, even with the archness in which my poor father attempted to hide the essential viciousness and despair of the narrative.

"Once upon a time," said my father, seated in his wheel chair, and summoning unknowingly in that traditional opening the continuous present necessary to the interest of any story, "Once upon a time," he repeated, "an old farmer named Schrecklichkeitunendlich" (a name chosen to tickle me) "and his young son Hans, aged ten, went to town taking with them their brown pony named Ego." "Ego, Father?" I asked. "That is a strange name for a pony or anyone else." "No, no," said my bitter father, "it is a well-known name." "I have never heard of anyone with that name," I said stubbornly. "Please," said my father, angered, "if you continue to interrupt me, I will never finish the story, which you begged me to tell you. Father, son, and pony," my father continued, "started for the market place, and Hans rode the pony. It was a beautiful blue-and-gold day in the month of June, and all three were pleased with all things, the father because he was going to sell the pony and with the proceeds buy a gun with which to kill deer, the son because he had been promised a pair of boxing gloves by the father, and the pony merely glad because he was exercising himself and the weather was fine.

"The three travelers had gone but a mile—the town being four miles distant—when a man with a whip came along from the opposite direction, and seeing them, said indignantly: 'O pitiless boy! You who are young and strong ride the pony, while your father, the weak old man, walks beside you and by such exertion shortens his days. Get down from the pony, let your father ride, honor your father, remember his weakness.' Intimidated by this, father and son said nothing, the traveler went on his way absentmindedly, Hans dismounted, and his father mounted the pony."

"But they should have had two ponies," I said to my father. "They had only one," my father replied. "The number of ponies is not infinite. Many people have only one pony, and as for us, as you know, we have none," said my father in his embittered voice and continued.

"They went forward another mile and another stranger approached, holding a gun in his hand, stopped them, took the pony by the halter, standing there as if he were an official authority: 'Evil old man,' he said. 'Selfish father! The young boy must walk while the father rides, as if he were a king and would like to live forever.'"

"A king, Father?" I inquired. "Kings do not live forever. No one does." "By king, I meant an important person," he said annoyed and impatient. "Do not, please, interrupt me so often.

"The stranger stood there so threateningly that the father dismounted. Satisfied, the stranger passed on, leaving father and son completely perplexed, not knowing at all what to do. Suddenly Hans was inspired: 'Father, Father!' he said. 'We will both ride the pony.' The father saw how intelligent this idea was and said with pride: 'Hans, you are a smart boy,' and soon both were mounted on the pony and jogging toward town. The pony's pace slowed up a bit, but not otherwise did he show himself troubled by the additional weight.

"But soon a third stranger came along, saw them and stopped them. This one brandished a sword and said, in a tone of the greatest moral indignation and self-righteousness: 'O heartless humans! Both of you riding one weak and young pony! What ruthless cruelty toward the dumb and inoffensive beast! Dismount before you kill him, or I will report you to both the civil and sacred authorities!' Both father and son dismounted hurriedly, and clumsily (for it is difficult for two to dismount from a horse at the same time). 'Something is always wrong,' said the father aloud, as he dismounted and the stranger, satisfied, departed.

" 'Hans,' said the father, 'we will both walk and the pony will walk beside us. Then perhaps all will be content.' No sooner had he said this than a fourth stranger appeared. Hans drew back and wished to hide in the wood until the stranger passed, especially since the newcomer carried a whip, *and* a gun, *and* a sword. But the father decided against hiding. 'What is wrong with you?' said the stranger in a voice whose kindliness stunned them with surprise. 'Why don't you ride the pony? Why are you so stupid? What is a pony for, if not to ride?' Then the stranger passed on, before they could tell him of the difficulties involved in riding the pony.

"Desperate by this time, the farmer said: 'Son, only one choice remains. If either of us ride the pony, we will remain at the mercy of these denunciations of the first, second, and third class. We must carry the pony, then perhaps all sides will be satisfied.' 'The pony may not like it, Father.' 'He is silent. If he says anything, we will whip him.' And so they lifted the pony on their backs, although it was a difficult and clumsy thing to do."

"Father," I said at this point, in disbelief, "you are inventing this story. You ought not to tell me falsehoods. No one carries a pony upon his back. That is ridiculous." My father was greatly angered and slapped me savagely, making me howl with pain. "Don't ever call your father a liar," he said. "It's enough that your mother does so."

"Finish the story, Father, please," I said meekly, weeping.

"After a slow and painful effort, the farmer and Hans managed to reach the market place, carrying the pony upon their backs and looking very strange. In the market place, idlers were congregated, who, when they saw this sight, began to laugh and their laughter increased in intensity and volume. 'What are you good-for-nothings laughing about?' said the father, challenging them, while Hans in shame hid his head in his father's sleeve. The leader, the biggest wiseacre of all, answered: 'Why, you damned fool! Whoever heard of carrying a pony? A pony is supposed to carry you.' Their laughter increased still more at this sally, and the farmer felt completely helpless—at the end of his rope—and besides he could not stand being laughed at, being very sensitive. So he took out his revolver, which he had had in his pocket all the while, and—bang! bang! bang!—shot the pony, shot his son, and, shrugging his shoulders, and brushing the hair back from his forehead, shot himself."

My mother entered at this moment and began to argue with my father for telling the child such a story, and soon all the hate between them made each bring up past wrongs on each other's part, and in their heat they forgot my presence and spoke shamelessly and brutally, while I wept loudly, watching them, weeping because of the sad end of the story, because they were denouncing each other and because I had been slapped for calling my father a liar.

Over the soft pudding of my face
I passed my hand to assure myself of where
My place was, where my gaze and gazing mind:
The warm bath of awareness mounts again.
His story was my story, he was I,
Myself divided in identity,
Dressed in a dress suit, seated secretly
Where all my studied ghosts surrounded me.

Now has the hero come to get his prize
—The Senate's gift and office.
                      Waiting there
(The while the well-coached crowd approaches him,
As yet unheard),
                 Marcius makes inquiries
About Aufidius, his perfect foe,
Necessitous to him.
                  The day, the joy,
The glory and circumstance of honor
Hardly concern him (all taken for granted,
Being achieved)
               but with what interest he
Hears how Aufidius bears him full hate,
Wishes a cause to seek him out once more,
Strive with him once for all
                  and kill him!
—Affirms the dogma of his being thus.

The tribunes come, pretend to warn him,
                           he
Perceives their plot, denounces them,
                        asserts
That all concessions only
Increase class conflict and unite the poor,

Raising their appetite:
                        "He's right," says Marx,
Absorbed beside me.
                        Brutus and Velutus
Provoke him more, knowing their man full well,
Mention a scandal long forgot, scratch hard
All of his paining skin,
                        until his choler,
Indulged like a thirst, mouthed with bulging eyes,
Alienates everyone on every side.

—O apoplectic then, he speaks as if
For his own class, but they, patricians there,
Standing beside him, censure him, regret
His utterance, perceive his drunkenness,
And seek to soothe all partisans.
                        He howls
A theory of the state, he calls the people
Hydra, a monster, he requires the Senate
To end the tribunes' power,
                        he insists
That they take on his spirit and his humor
—While they, not fed as he, stand coldly by,
Outside his passion, moved to pure distaste,
Trying to quiet him, take him away.

At which he blazes! All not with him
Are against him!
                        "Enough, enough!"
Menenius says;
                        "Traitor!" the tribunes cry,
"O not enough! Take more!" Narcissus howls,
"That many-headed monster must be strapped,
His tongues plucked out and every loud inch whipped.
Erect! O noblemen, be not debased,
They are the Senators, you are displaced!"
But no response. But he is quite alone,
Foreign, alien, estranged.

The crowd arrives,
Whipped on by Brutus.
                    "Arrest him now,"
Brutus demands. "The city is the people"
("The city is the people," the people echo),
"And he their enemy, let him be killed,
Borne to the rock Tarpeian and cast down!"
Thus the deliberate tribune asks his death,
"Tarpeian death, hurled from the naked rock,
Forth from the falling sky to rising ruin."
And the poor people, whipped on by the tribunes,
Echo their voices, move to seize the hero.

—Whereat he draws his sword, himself unsheathed,
And still defies them.
                    "Down with that sword,"
Menenius cries. "Lay hands on him,"
Brutus demands.
                    The Senate's guard arrives,
Briefly the crowd is beaten back,
Marcius is hurried elsewhere by his friends.

The orchestra resumes. Beethoven blows
The raw emotion through the passive air
As through the body's darkness. Well he knows
(And well the violins are sworded there)
Responsive anger savage in the head,
Hammered and stammered till its fist is fed.

"This man," murmurs the Stagirite to me,
"Breaks down the categories. Every man
Divided by them, yet a surd remains,
Himself and not his genus, species, class,
And not his time, his place, his quantity:
Something remains,
                    each man a quality,
As is the color, blue, the taste of, sweet,
Indivisible, individual, alone,

But of all personal animals
Marcius is most extreme, most radical,
Discolors with his teeth each element,
Which gave him being, cooks it, pukes it up,
So by transforming all, himself to be,
Though vomiting be all activity,
Till in the vomit's tint and smell he sees
His unique essence living as disease."

"O as disease indeed!" Marx intervenes,
"See what a fracture such uniqueness means!
He who would rend himself from his own class
Shall feel his self ragged as broken glass."

"His mother's breast," intrudes the Viennese,
"Delighted him too much, fixed his disease.
The child misunderstood, blind animal:
Dark Id rules all, and though impersonal,
Fixed to the womb this individual:
'O Mutter, Mutter, it is cold outside':
So speaks his wish to die, such is his pride."

"O no!" Karl Marx insists. "You do not see
His veritable mother, the genuine She
From whom he sucked his pieties, his mind
His sword, his words, his war, his unchewed rind,
His anger, his desires. She is here
Near to him as his hands and feet are near!"

The house of Marcius now. The living room.
—Nobles convened to meet their class's woe.
All members of the ruling class.
They speak as such, adjudge his character
And find him wanting too, or rather too
Abnormal, alien, foreign, strange, a freak,
Not of their kind, though they admire him
As one admires the sun, shading his eyes.

"He is too noble for the world," says one,
"He is a god or beast, he is the one
Whom Aristotle in his *Politics*
Refers to as apart from any city,
Not one to live in a community,
Superior or inferior to the state,
Disdains the shadow which he treads at noon,
And would not flatter God for what is His,
No, would not recognize the Deity
—The only one perfect and all alone."

Enter Cominius with word that now
The wound can still be bandaged, the people
Pacified
        (forgiving, forgetful, relative),
The people will pardon him,
                        if he but
Affirm the people's rights, the tribune's office
And show such courtesy as strangers get
To those who will be dogs if they are pets
—Who merely wish to sit down and be friends.

His friends plead with him, kindly, carefully,
Call on his loyalty, ask that but once,
That he but once not make his mouth his heart,
Or civil war and the class war will burn,
Or he will die.
                And thus they touch him not,
Or rather butter the obelisk, his callous height,
For he invites Tarpeian death, insists
That ten times worse will never alter him,
Nor height a million times as high as is
The rock Tarpeian change his attitude
And make him politic.
                        O in New York
His swollen heart would find true properties!
We have such pyramids as financiers

Descend when their arithmetic's full sum
Betrays a debt the smashing pavement pays.

One puny qualm he has: "I muse my mother
Does not approve me further."
                              So he says
As she appears, appeals to her at once.
His only audience:
                    "Am I not true,
Mutter, am I not true to my own nature?"
In baby lisp requesting flattery.

But she, annoyed and firm, and not as he,
Calls him too foolish, yes, a very child,
One who would eat his cake before he has it,
And show his private parts in company.

"I am as you," she says, though she is not,
"As proud, contemptuous, intransigent,
But with an adult mind and not a child's,
Prudent, reasonable,
                      O go," she says,
"Repent to the tribunes."
                          "No," he says.
"You are too absolute," she cries, "beg, kneel,
Tell them you have a soldier's violent tongue."
"No, no," he says, although already moved,
"I cannot change my face"—such is his claim—
"Revise my heart, no, not for God himself,
How then for them?
                    The unwashed stinking horde!"
"I beg you," says Volumnia, "I do,
Sweet son!"
            "O well!" thus he consents, consents
And calls himself a whore, describes consent
With such disgust that he offends himself,
Reneges again, refuses, stricken by
His grimace in the glass of his own voice.

Her anger mounts. "You are an absolute,
You recognize not mother, wife, nor child,
Nor any relative. You are alone."
—Never before as harsh!
                              Denies her still,
Though in the streets the crowds are packed, and wait,
Till she tugs wholly at the silver cord.
—First for the city and his own friends' sake,
The ground on which he stands, from which he rose;
Then, knowing, intuitive, she says she is
The senators, the city, his son, his wife
(Freud bursts to speak beside me), she unites
All in one picture, She, enormous mother,
All stimuli, all bells, and every cue.

—Still he denies, although with weakening face,
Still she pursues, cries out in rage that she
Pays for the insane pride sucked from her breast,
Pays for the ego which her womb fed well,
Which now pre-empts all things, thinks all is his.

"Chide me no more!" Marcius, consenting, hurt,
Obedient to the womb's authority:
"I'll be a mountebank, an easy whore
Who sleeps with every sex and every lie,
Perjure myself, juggle their jogging hearts
With my sweet temper, kiss each pimpled face,
Answer their perjury with my own honor,
And come back Consul—perfectly forgiven!"
"O what an *animal!*" says Aristotle;
"How torn by contradictions!" says Karl Marx,
"O as a girl finds heavy in her self
And bigger day by day, more obvious,
That joy's commission which shall be her shame,
So does the ton of evil in this man
Move to denouement, issue, tragedy.
As a society contains within itself
The child which shall destroy it, so does he

Nurse in his breast the striving love and hate
Which shall annul him!"
                    "O he yields," says Freud,
"To childhood's queen, that is, his very mother!"
"Not to Volumnia," Karl Marx replies,
"But to the mother obsessing all men's eyes!
His biggest mother toward his much-used breast!
Fame is her face, economy her bone,
No man departs from her and lives alone!"
"A man may go away," says Plato's son,
"Travel beneath the moon until he has won
Virtue, knowledge, the good. Wherever he goes
One mother shadows him and shows
Prior to him in actuality
—As his mind's words, his warm identity!"

Now at the Forum, Brutus and Velutus
Coach the poor people, prompt their will, dictate
Their act, prepare to provoke their Marcius,
Knowing him well, to self-destroying anger,
Any pretext or wound.
                    He comes before them,
A staring audience which shows as if
The city painted its own image there.
The tribunes question him and he replies
Adequately, gravely, quietly,
Acknowledges the people's rights.
                            His friends
Chime in, apologize, call this enough,
The meeting verges on its happy end
—Yet he cannot suppress a single query,
Why he's been crowned and then crudely uncrowned
Within an hour?
                Seizing their chance, the tribunes
Accuse him,
        call him traitor!
                        charge his will
Of tyranny and kingship!

                        False and true,
His rage explodes immediately! He
Defies them, frenzied, his tongue hysterical,
Defies a million deaths from them.
                                    The people,
Prompted, pulled by a string or button, roar.
"Exile or death?" the tribunes quickly ask.
"Exile!" the people roar,
While Marcius foams, spitting every curse:
"I exile you!" he cries. "Your breath I hate!
I banish you. There is a world elsewhere."
Thus does the king, falsely accused, enact
His empty kingship, striking his own heart,
While the poor people praise their worthy voices,
Wishing a little good and to be friends.

Here I am once more, dressed in a toga to suit the occasion. I am sure you will agree that this performance is nothing, if not engrossing. Surely the consequences will provide that fine thing, *katharsis*, concerning which one member of the audience has long been an expert; *katharsis* equal and even superior to that of the sexual act, which begins everything and ends nothing, and often, as everyone knows, produces as aftermath the most unutterable sadness, even in those so self-delighting that they are intoxicated by the comeliness of their own shadows.

I do not doubt that my appearance here is questionable. Why, you may ask, does this voluble intruder come upon the stage and interrupt the occasion with what he seems to regard as of interest to us? Let me confess, in reply, that I am not very sure of what I am saying, but that I have a grave need of speech which I can justify to myself. My reason, my justification is the fact that I am here. Since I am here, it would be well for you to hear what I have to say. If I remained silent, you might be deceived as to what you are seeing. Let the observer be observed by all observers in the act of observing what there is to observe. May I confess, however, that I am not sure of this justification itself. It is very difficult to be sure of anything. Let us, however, rather risk foolishness than permit any fact to remain obscure.

To continue with my memoirs, there was a city. That city occupied a place near the sea. Historians disagree as to the reason for choosing this place. Some say that an old father committed incest with his daughter and came here, seeking a certain strangeness for his new family. Some, however, insist that men came from across the sea seeking precious metals on this coast and remained here because they were tired. Thirdly, it is said that this community was founded because the sea provided a means of commerce with other nations from whom desirable commodities could be obtained. Lastly, there are some who speak with certainty of their belief that an indolent pleasure-seeking man chose this place because he was pleased by views of the sea and also admired the countryside and enjoyed the climate. All agree, however, that the decision which brought the first one to this place to begin the city was his own desire; whatever that desire may have been, he was seeking its satisfaction.

The time soon came when the beginning was obscure and unconsidered, apart from the fact of desire. The owners of ships were the most important men in this community. This was because ships carried from other nations the commodities deemed to be necessary or desirable. As a result, the building of ships was very important. Such matters occupied both the educational system and the games of the children. In order to make the ships, it was necessary above all to cut down forests for wood. The neighboring countryside was abundantly forested. Equally important was the craft of making a ship, and great honor was paid to the shipbuilder. The commodities brought from other nations were paid for, in general, either by a shipment of lumber or by completely made ships. This led to numerous conflicts. The shipowners protested against the sale of ships to other nations in too great a quantity because it deprived them of their commercial advantage. The owners of the ships and the owners of the forests attempted to profit by the needs of each other. After a time, a crisis arose as a result of the fact that the neighboring forests were depleted. Consequently, many became aware of the relationship of the city to Nature. Another region of forests was acquired further inland, but after a time this too was completely cut down, and it became necessary to make war upon a distant city to obtain additional forests. The result of each crisis was that first the making and the owning of ships was seized by one group of owners and later shipbuilding, shipping, and the ownership of forests all became the ownership of one group, the group which at first had merely owned ships.

In this city there was a boy who lived a personal life in which at every given opportunity he judged, that is to say, evaluated the kind of being and the ways of life which surrounded him. Such judging was natural to him, made him lonely, sprang from his desire to know what he might enact, possess, and attain when he was permitted to choose, if he were permitted to do so. Such judging was as much a matter of his body's intuitive responses as of a conscious effort to decide what various objects and processes were worth to him. He strolled by the seaside, regarded the sea, the ships in the harbor, the sailors washing the decks. He walked on the great avenue where stood the big houses of the rich merchants, the owners of ships. He gazed with no little curiosity into their windows, striving to see if life had a different quality there. He looked long into the display windows of the shopkeepers, where were shown all the goods which had been obtained from many nations. He studied the diamonds in the jeweller's window, and observed that a thing of intrinsic goodness had a certain toughness. He sat in the waiting room of a doctor and saw that many were ill for a long time and he stood where tickets were bought for journeys and knew that many wish to go away and many return. He cracked the nuts given him by a grocer, ate the meat contained in them, decided that it would be foolish to consider eating a major satisfaction. He made the acquaintance of a druggist who permitted him to try his salves and ointments. He found them delicate. When, however, the druggist used his own cosmetics and simpered toward him, he fled, astonished by the arbitrary nature of taste. From a close vantage point, he gazed upon the sailors with their whores in the bushes near the driveway, and he knew that the body desires to penetrate and exhaust and make fat the body of another. A dentist told him that teeth were near the ego. He met metaphysicians who discussed the sea and painters who painted ships, but he was not as yet impressed. He met a theologian who told him that since all men must die, he would be foolish to concern himself with the practical arrangements of life, but wise to prepare himself with a decent character for the event of immortality. He spoke with an undertaker who told him that one must make a living and that in time one became used to everything. He observed children and saw how cruel they were in their games and knew that only later among a few adults who had escaped from childhood could one expect kindness, charity, an exact awareness of the torture and the tenderness of the ego. He saw how those who had authority were corrupted by the mere formality of their offices. During this prolonged examination he was by himself, had no friends, was regarded by his family as worse than useless. So great was his interest, however, that nothing deterred him, no one offended him by contempt, not even his father, who helped to build ships.

Boys who were clever or ambitious in this city were told to become builders of ships. If one were fortunate, courteous, hard-working, and extremely intelligent, one might attain to the privilege of sleeping with the daughters of the great merchants, the owners of ships. Boys were told that life was very sweet in their great houses as their sons-in-law. Then, by natural succession, one might hope to become oneself an owner of ships and forests, and a lord among the men of the city, walking in the assurance of all who possess themselves and inspire meekness, strict attention, admiring glances.

But he rejected these brilliant promises. They were not enough and they were already exemplified by young men of thinning hair and slight paunch who seemed to be endeavoring to remember what they had desired. He rejected the notion of hierarchy or stair implicit in this scheme. The rich did not seem to him to be at the top of the stair and the poor striving to climb at least one more flight. When he had reached this conclusion, however, he met an old sailor who argued that the people in the city were detained in a prison, the prison of the way in which each made his living and all secured the goods deemed necessary or desirable. The old sailor said that the objects of attention were dictated by this fact; conscious life was preoccupied and not free; the attitudes toward Nature were determined by the operation of instruments in the fields and on the water; the relationship between a man and his brother was determined by each one's function and no man's heart. Yet, said the old sailor, this is what at the beginning was desired, although no more. The honorable, the justifiable, the notable, the beautiful were dictated by a center of feeling which was itself merely a narrow response to the manifold forms of the way in which each good in general was made, secured, kept, taken and given. The boy was shocked to hear this, and disturbed by the old sailor's advice, namely, to go to sea and to seek among the rocking scenes of indeterminacy a certain freedom of feeling, also freedom from the ways of the city. This seemed to him merely the counsel of evasion and escape. A pause occurred in which his decisive response prepared itself. It would be like no other man's, since no one had lived the days which he had lived. He had seen many desires and satisfactions and been somewhat impressed by all of them. No one of them failed to enter into the new and unique center of feeling which prepared itself in his heart; just as the muscles of the runner have been minutely determined by his daily rounds about the track, so that even the cinders and the airs of early morning have affected them and entered into their very being.

This boy was at the moment of falling in love and all the love he had seen was present in him, though differently. All men are in love, the forms of love are many: such was the knowledge present in him. As his first enactment of the long fate of love, he went to sea and in this act was contained the potentialities of the future of the city. For he discovered a new land of forests and thus from his original longing transformed the shipbuilding of the city and thus in the end its way of life. Or he discovered a new means of moving ships and transformed the commerce of the city. His new center of feeling, though derived from the city, made it necessary for him to murder the captain of the ship in order that he might proceed in the ways of his own origination. Let us depart from him, even as he departs from the city on his voyage toward himself and the future. See him! He stands at the prow, observing the glittering possibilities of the waters as the ship moves forward in time. He is in love. I am in love with him!

SCENE ONE

Lifting his silly nightgown up,
My twin retires once more; I am once more
Beside myself. I feel myself
Behind my face, quiet as moonlight is,
Pale gilt within the night.
                              His utterance,
Jejune and lyrical, is mine, my own.
He tells my secrecy, my private mind,
My very heart in accents crude and broad,
And I am gratified to have it known
(Let it be known, I think, that is my pleasure,
Let it be fully known, if it is true,
Of every mind with technique mine alone
Sleeps such a dream, endures this brutal night),
But shamed by his voluble nakedness.

The parting scene comes now. Now at the gate
Marcius commences exile, separates
From mother, wife, and son, from friends and Rome
(A few patricians, the imitative young,
Entranced by him, are also there),
Dismisses tears and their extended arms,
Limp attitudes of farewell and of grief
—And though Cominius would go with him
For a full month until he's once more rooted
("But what are men," says Plutarch, "plants, to stay
Fixed in one place? The mind's a traveler,
The wandering mind which makes us moving souls,"
So says one ghost by me, equivocal),
Marcius refuses. He would go alone
Like a lonely dragon, so he says,
Telling them that they soon will hear of him

121

And what they hear will be but as before
The future like the past as one stone like
Another stone in hardness.
                              The city is a beast,
A many-headed beast which butts him hence,
Or so he says, wholly unmodified.
"A beast, indeed! His mother is a beast,
Great womb, great height, great strength," says one late ghost.

"Mother, my letters will be regular.
I am sufficient, I will be myself."
Though he to the audience seems precarious,
Sinking in quicksand or the soft of water
Or trembling on a perilous height, in fact
("All men are sometime acrobats,
Or tight-rope walkers, teetering their strut"),
He to himself is strong, the tough Narcissus
Rather takes pleasure in this exile's wound,
And thinks it shows him perfect once again,
Reaches again for that sweet solitude
When he walked home alone from school, when he
Was the whole world in his mother's womb.

"The navel-cord is cut!" the Marxian cries,
"The belly-button bleeds! The hero dies!
Thus will he pay the dialectical price;
Each virtue when too swollen is a vice!
O with what blindness he departs from Rome!"

Beethoven's tears accompany the poem.

CHOOSE

No introduction, no idle remarks, I am tired as you of too much discussion and come now merely to bring the story forward.

Marcius, having departed from Rome went from place to place. He spoke to no one, he knew no one, he had no place to go, he ate and slept alone, and he had only his sense of hatred and of appalling injury, the savage anger which obsessed his revery, only this passion, to occupy the lucid day of many objects and the vague night when nothing exists. No purpose, no desire, except the vindictive appetite, nothing of which to think but his past victories and his uncontrollable longing to smash certain faces, which made him clench his fists merely, as he proceeded on his journey to no end.

At first he was gratified in his unceasing walk because he was alone with his towering shadow, which compared itself with nothing, either in the sterile desert or the cool forest. And at first he was gratified by the strange bedrooms in which he was alone with his own smell, the only one which did not offend him. Soon he was less pleased and a blister on his foot made him feel an incomparable pity for himself. Later he was annoyed because he had no one to speak to, except the one whom he asked for something to eat and a place to sleep. Meanwhile he still considered himself completely independent and was under the impression that he was proving his self-sufficiency. One night, however, he dreamed that he had returned to Rome, recanted, unsaid his pride, and begged their forgiveness, asked to be killed or permitted to remain, the least of citizens in Rome, traveling a greater number of miles each day in order to deny the dream and convince himself that what occurred in the prone passivity of sleep had nothing to do with himself awake. Stiff-necked, hardening his heart, hating the need which sleep disclosed, he came at last, after the worst despair, to a lake ringed by pines after a long journey in a barren and flat terrain. It was a perfect day in the middle of September. The lake sparkled a million times and the soft wind crossed the shuffled, shuffling waters. The night before, he had dreamed the identical dream of returning and begging forgiveness. He has come to despise his sleep and to be afraid of not remaining awake. Desolate, desolate. Even his mother against him, even his sleep betraying him, even his hatred become ambiguous; Narcissus, Brutus, Judas, knowing no place to go, having no desire, attained to the emptiness for which he had striven, sick at heart more than ever before he kneels by the water, bends over it, and then, staring at the water, kneeled above it, he sees his own face there, folded over and over, distorted under the ripple, undulating, and he coughs! amazed to hear the sound of his body in the silence, sneezes! in a sudden chill, in his body's weakness and disbelief. He sees his face, his thick lips, curly hair, flaring nostrils, broad forehead. His haunted eyes regard themselves, round lakes full of a kind of sweat. They still get pleasure from their own unmoved look. He is somewhat aware of the rippling water, and of the sky, the eternal gem, reflected therein, a curious hat or backdrop for his head.

It is the moment of vision and decision. Staring upon that face which is his own, he sees his own life, and the lives rejected and the choices chosen, and the immediacy of anger and pleasure, and the abstracted stare of memory, and the strangeness, to himself, of his own face, the most peculiar of flowers.

And then his mother's face replaces his own and blooms until it has become an enormous image, quivering or trembling in the water or in the sky. She looks at him as if she were waiting for him to speak to her and he gazes back, afraid and yet unable to turn away, trying to believe what he sees before him, whether in the water or the sky. And then, as if decided that he will not speak to her, she says to him:

"You cannot depart from me. You are nothing apart from me, you do not exist without me. I will be with you no matter where you go. Your lips are mine, your globe-like head and your deep body, your swinging arms, your strength, system and urge, habit, complexion, and dress. I fed you. I gave you each part of your being, or you took that part from me. The word of your tongue is mine. Your effort to depart from me is your pain, your evil. I am your mother or Rome. I am Volumnia or Rome.

"But I am yours. You are your own; lips, face, hair, look, your own, your property. This is your freedom. You are free, self-choosing, a king. Your words are yours, although they are mine. Although you have taken yourself from me, nevertheless your speech is your choice, your life is your making, your being is your own. Nothing compels you, no imperative dictates to you, the actuality of your choice is what it is for you, your individuality grasps the uniqueness of each moment. This surpasses me. This is your freedom. Choose!"

Act Four:
"A Goodly House, the Feast Smells Well"

SCENE TWO

Inveterate, gratuitous, too much,
Ambiguous, I tire even myself.

—The curtain rises on a night in which
All's indeterminate except the moon,
Marcius in white, and two enormous signs,
Painted in phosphorus at right and left
As if alternatives were parts of place
And choice a bird which whirls upon the air
And comes to rest
                    only to rise once more,
To ANTIUM, at left, as advertised;
To ROME, at right, and Marcius in between
Outstretched upon the ground.
                                    Night over all
Except the rounding moon which dreams of snow,
Unnatural as both signs.
                          "Don't," he says,
Prone there upon the ground as if in bed
In possibility, "won't, cannot, must not,
Deny the coercive heart.
                          Friendship is green,
The hearth is glowing. Man cannot live alone,
That world is colorless, an infinite gray,
Nothing to do, nothing to wish and act,
Dance in a vacuum to no audience,
And no applause,
                  But they hurt me, hit me,
Whispered behind my back and shut the door,
Nobles as well as poor. And no one said,
'O no, he is our friend, shall stay with us,
Eat at our table and play games with us,

Till the mob stone our children and our house.'
No one in Rome said this—
                              bone, stone, unknown,
Thrown and alone—
                    I'll go to Antium,
Seek out Aufidius, my worst enemy;
He and his friends be my good company,
My heart's my own!
                    I choose myself, I'll die
Crying to Rome its fate, that I am I!"

"This is the turning-point," said Aristotle,
"This the peripety, he now has done
All that a man can do, committed his will
Once and for all, purchased his only fate.
He's helpless now, as one who, stepping, falls,
The rest is his great chute, descent, career."
"Every act is a boomerang," says Freud,
"A ricochet, a knife which cuts the butcher."
"This man still eats his heart," Beethoven said,
"It is a pretty dish and he will starve:
Chords spread upon the air their synthesis
Of all that is involved within the kiss,
Her lips the curved soft fruit of blood, her breath
Excitement's rhythm, quite aware of death.
How many actualities pass by unnamed,
Music anonymous shall witness this,
Music essentially vague shall wholly tell
With what variety man goes to hell!"

Now Jew is silent and the Greek is still,
Bent over the fate of that sad animal.
While I, I am afraid of that fifth ghost
Who is unknown, who has not said one word.

A scene that's quickly done. Marcius before
The house of Aufidius in Antium.
In mean apparel, muffled and disguised,

Regards the sour twilight and the city,
A handsome city to his exiled gaze,
One which has suffered many a widow from him,
Hearsed many an heir too soon.

                                        He asks the street
Where great Aufidius stays, wholly aware
How times have changed, how dialectical
His straight heart turns the curving world.
He vows his love to Antium, his hate to Rome.

A hall in the house of great Aufidius.
Music within blooms with its order and love,
Radiant, resolving all voices in its own
He enters hesitant and wholly muffled;
The sound of banqueting

                                        strikes at his heart,
Music and food, mutual being, three
Baskets or contexts by which man's heart is kept
From falling through nothingness.

                                        Where Marcius stands
An angle of the dining room is seen
And three men's faces show at the long table,
Eating and laughing, caught unknowingly
In two dual aims, to eat and yet guffaw.

"The feast smells well. But I am not a guest."
Marcius instructs himself,

                                        he hears the clink
Of glasses met, the brittle tap of fork
Against the plate;

                        sudden, an active hush
While one would tell a story of their fellow,
Until at the sweet crux, all roar,

                                        even,
The silly fool whose foolishness is told
Glad to be famous there and then and thus.
—Wishes himself that fool, himself unfed,
As a servant enters crying, "Wine! Wine!"

127

Wine that the warm glow of company
May be sustained, renewed, increased to blaze.

The servant sees him, the servant as the snob
Sees his mean dress, asks with impudence
Just what he wants.
                "Aufidius," he replies,
Telling himself that he deserves no welcome
Other than this.
             A second servant joins;
Both, being a little drunk and hi-de-ho,
Refuse to call Aufidius, abuse him.
"Get out before I throw you out," says one;
"Sure, you're a pretty guest," the other says.
"Where do you live?" they ask.
                   Marcius replies,
"Under the sky, under the canopy!
With crows, with eagles, with vultures, and with God!"
"Get out! This is no place for you!" they cry,
Pushing him roughly,
               bringing his choler
Until he jaws at them with old contempt
And the row brings in Aufidius.
                  His name
(Not recognizing him in his mean dress)
Aufidius requires. He
With a slight pun of hesitation
Calls himself *Caius Marcius*, then, wholly,
Coriolanus, bursts out his whole history—
All pride, rancor, rage against Rome,
The cruelty and envy of the people
And how the bastard nobles all forsook him—
Offers himself unto Aufidius,
As victim, or as friend to knock down Rome.
"Most absolute sir!" just as his mother did,
Aufidius welcomes him. "Come in, come in!"
He jubilates, joy overbrims. "Come in!
This is a second wedding night for me;

Shake hands with all and eat and drink with us,
Welcome a million times! For your own sake
Will we tear Rome to pieces! Marcius, come in!"

The servants too rejoice that war is come,
While the hubbub rises from the dining room,
For war, says one, in fact unites all men,
While peace makes cuckolds, peace makes idleness,
Boredom and quietness.
                        "When peace rules us
Men have no need of friendship, therefore sleep,
Quarrel, grow old, insensible and stupid."

A public place in Rome. The tribunes speak
Of Marcius' absence and the city's peace.
Rome fattens, rid of its poor absolute;
All's well, the people sing at work,
Or so the tribunes say.
                        Even Menenius
Admits the happiness, regrets that Marcius
Could never temporize, reports that none,
Nor mother, wife, nor he, knows where he is,
Has heard from him.
                        Citizens pass, profess
Their grateful ease and thank the useful tribunes
Who now judge Marcius once again, repeat
That though brave soldier, he was arrogant,
Proud, ambitious past imagination,
Self-loving, harsh, wished to be king of Rome.

And as they speak, amid their sleek content,
News shakes them, shocks them:
                        Coriolanus!
Coriolanus leads the Volscian host!
Ravishes colonies and comes toward Rome!
Terror rises. Panic
Seizes the populace. The patricians
Hurry to meet
                and fear convulses all!

And now the Volscian camp. As he shakes Rome,
He gnaws Aufidius with every tooth,
Unknowingly, though vowed to show, in all,
Humility, and move with modesty,
And loyalty.
               But the true surd
Is irreducible. The individual
Is uncontrollable. To him, to him
The soldiers draw, forget Aufidius,
Render him virtual kingship.

Aufidius is deathly jealous. "He is,
He is," he says, "by nature but one thing,
Cannot be otherwise, cannot deny
His nature more than a triangle can.
For this was he banished, and for this
—So virtue lies in circumstance alone,
And every time interprets us—
                     becomes
The idol of all hearts, the man I kill!"

The orchestra begins. Bomb! Bomb! Bomb!
Rome and her strangest child in double harm!
Evil is complex. Though man walk alone
He steps upon the whole world
                     and is thrown!

HE IS A PERSON

Ladies and Gentlemen, here I am for the last time, dressed as a knight in armor in order to recall the days when our fathers thought they understood good and evil and old Nobodaddy (concerning whom I intend to remain silent). I would venture to say that this performance was near its conclusion. Conclusion, however, is a fiction, in fact, for we know neither beginning nor end, only the report of them. For we are always in the middle of everything, and our lives are, need I say, infinitely divisible; like Achilles and the tortoise, we shall never get home, and I, a veritable Coleridge, must buttonhole you once more, the most belated Shakespearean fool.

Here I am finally to provide you with an abstract picture postcard of the wounded nudity about which all things whirl, that is to say, the soul. In the Shakespearean night, the souls of the poor fool and the brave hero and the gentle lady shiver and huddle in a nakedness which no dress covers. In the precise center of this oblong postcard a human being is shown, possessing hair, eyes, hands, feet, arms, belly, genitals, and the other parts which make possible thought, movement, and love. This human being might be mistaken for Joseph, who had a many-colored coat; Moses, for whom God burned; David, who threw stones so well; Ulysses, who wished to go home; Orestes, who was hunted; Oedipus, who destroyed his own eyesight (perhaps secretly desiring the vision of Tiresias); Peter, betrayed by the cock; Dante, the greatest traveler; or the remorseless Morning Star, John Milton, who seduced our first mother. He might be mistaken for any one of these famous gentlemen. For look you! he undergoes that pain of all vertebrates, the labor of standing up. He endures the loneliness of all conscious beings. He ties his shoelaces in his own style, which merely shows that like those famous heroes, he is betrayed by his body, his feet hurt him and he must blow his nose. In his own style, he ties his shoelaces, and enacts the other motions which distinguish his identity amid the infinite host. He adjusts his hat and his tie before the oval mirror in the hallway in his own inimitable idiom. His uniqueness is obvious, though he resembles other members of his family. His voice has a certain intonation which has never been heard from another man. His step on the stairs and his key in the lock can be recognized as his. No one, not the most precise counterfeiter, can duplicate his handwriting, for no one writes with precisely such curls. His handwriting is, however, merely a symptom of his nervous system. He is original.

Now, as he stands there and moves toward himself, a breathing animal, almost divine, let us ask once more the question which we do not evade. Who is he? Let us begin again as we always begin again in order that we may continue. What is he? He is his father and his mother, neither of whom are represented on the postcard. He is his childhood, which is also absent. He is his adolescence, which is each one's *Vaterland*. He is his young manhood. Let us begin again. He is his fatherland, which is his adolescence, and he is his mother, which is his childhood. None of this can be represented upon the postcard, and you, when you look at any man, remember that you do not truly see him. For he is his past and his past is unseen, although it is one of the greatest of powers. His past holds him and he must move forward in time, dragging every fear and every beauty of every year with him. They will never release him! He carries his habits, which are his childhood, strapped to him like his wrist watch, beating.

And he moves, because he must, and thus he is betrayed to the unending agony of conscious being. Thus he moves forward to what he has not yet been. Here his pain awaits him and here he is as yet nothing. The repetition of yesterday and the day before will never suffice, but he must create again and again from what has been the unheard-of future. The future of time which is nothing cannot be grasped by the repetition of what has been. It is not enough. He must create what has never existed. The necessity of the future intrudes and he must choose, although as most often he merely chooses what has already existed. Such is the nothingness which faces him. He is the future. He is a person!

See him, in admiration and fear. Remark the original face which is unrecognizable, never before having been. Regard his face and suppose the unknown heart and the secret head, which create the nature of what is to come. The past is transformed in him. The world begins again. All is torn in him and altered in the richest exchanges. Passionate nonesuch, his heart consumes the world. His freedom breaks his heart. His freedom creates the future. He is the mystery, irreducible. His freedom is his mystery. With his freedom he does it, his unknown creative act. With that mystery, his own identity, he who will never have sufficient names, invents the future! O my beauty! See him, sharply and exactly. Coriolanus, Caius Marcius Coriolanus, Coriolanus, the individual.

Act Five:
"As If a Man Were Author of Himself"

That twin goes back: too much and not enough,
Led by the ecstasy of his tongue,
Hiding what wish and hope I do not know,
And by ideas possessed and tricked
By his imagination like an heir
Straining in mind unto a vast access
Upon a change as radical as death—
And I, by now accustomed to be twice,
And by their wits' tuition tossed side to side,
Hunger for what necessity has supplied.

The curtain rises on the heart of man
As always in America and Asia
But now on Rome in crisis.
                              Fear and dread
Tighten all people. As love makes one, so fear
Makes one; all have one will, one hope,
That Marcius, spewed out like a pit or rind,
Be sucked back by some intimate appeal,
His anger turned from them.
                              Cominius
Has been ambassador to him, returned,
And now reports the hapless interview:
—That Marcius would not answer; when he did,
Refused his name and called himself a nothing
Until a fire was his name,
                              Rome burning down!
"I kneeled before him," says Cominius,
"I called on every piety of his,
But like a metal his impervious face
—Then, faintly, he dismissed me, as if he spoke
Distant from me a thousand miles away!
—Only his mother might penetrate his hate."
Menenius, though demurring, is the next

134

Sent as ambassador—
                    to beg, solicit, plead,
All that auld lang syne may, in kneeling suit.
"—O," says Menenius, "I'll come to him
When he has had his dinner and fed well."
O plum, O filet mignon, charlotte russe,
Thus we depend on our immediacies,
Or so the old boy says.
                    The next scene shows
The Volscian host advanced, their general's tent,
Menenius arrived upon his mission,
Confronted by the soldier boy on guard:
"No visitors from Rome. *He* says *no one:*
None of his hometown boys can see him. You,
You treated him like dirt."
                    "Listen, I was,"
The old boy urges, "his best friend. We ate
And slept together!
                    Tell me, has my old chum
Had dinner yet? For I would speak to him
After he's had his coffee and dessert."
—As Marcius enters with Aufidius
To cry *Away* to *O my son! my son!*
And the ludicrous tears of fat Menenius:
"I have no wife, no mother and no child,
And if I knew you once, that is long past,
And now a nothingness is in between."
—Gives him, however, a letter of reprieve,
To save his person,
                    turns away, and asks
Aufidius to mark him obdurate,
Loyal and unattached by any string,
Chain, wire, or bond to Rome.
                    The soldiers watch
And call him noble, call their general
A rock perturbed by nothing in the world.
"Response! A man responds," says Sigmund Freud,
"Leaps back from that which strikes him, or falls down,

Departs, achieves a callous, or soars up,
Or goes to Africa or goes to wine,
A bird, a beast, a boxer, or he dies,
A fugitive,
        a sailor, tailor, jailer,
Barber or surgeon,
            all faces or replies
To the world's repeated fist, so various
And inescapable,
           questions or blows,
And a man responds, inventing every choice,
Adjusts, I say, with much imagination,
Seeks salves or runs away, gets bandages
And goes to sleep, makes speeches or denies
That that which is is what it is or seems,
Seems and is not,
             so this much-struck man now tries
A harder face each blow, a stranger answer,
A greater void, the womb, the wish to die——"

As mother, wife, and child in mourning clothes
Enter the tent of Coriolanus,
Muster all pathos, show very sad and meek,
Raise hands for his heart to take him down to them,
And stand in silence as our Marcius cries,
"Let me not be a father, husband, son!
Corrupt and rot, all warmth, affection, love!
Let nature die in me and instinct starve,
Their kneeling bodies be unmeaning blur!
O I will stand as stiff and staunch as stone,
As if a man were author of himself,
I will be author of myself alone!"
"It is the moment, Love," the Marxian cries,
"This man cuts every vine and so he dies!"
"Each would be God," exclaims the Stagirite,
"Desire has no top, is infinite!"

But, saying this, Coriolanus yields,

Yields slightly, kisses wife, and kneels
Before his kneeling mother, calls her best,
Best mother, his Olympus, his great height,
And is appalled to see his mother kneel,
The womb to drop down so.
                              Success's sweets,
It is the scene of Joseph satisfied,
The exile welcomed home on his own terms,
All lives within his will and whim.
                              Respond,
Respond, his mother means, showing to him
His only child, who is, she says, himself,
Will be as he, a needle of the sword,
And thus she rings all gongs to call him home.

"We sue for peace," Volumnia says,
Thinking the moment ripe and soft
—At which he freezes quite, begs them no plea,
Summons Aufidius and other Volscians
To see him still untouched.
                              Volumnia pleads.
"Again, again, we must see this again,"
So speaks the Viennese. "Mother and son,
The two exhausting their relationship,
A well-known fact of all communities
—Where's Hamlet and his Gertrude, Oedipus,
That ignorant man,
                    and Baudelaire?"
Volumnia speaks: "Rome is our nurse,
She suckles all of us. When you ruin Rome,
You tread your mother's womb, which made you real!"

"You tread my womb, which made a son for you,"
So speaks his wife.
                    And little Marcius cries,
"You will not tread on me. I'll run away
And fight when I get big!"
                              Amusing all

By this sheer mimicry of Marcius,
Rifting the serious a moment which
Gives Marcius difficulty with his face.

"All, all depends on him, on his sole heart.
He is contingency, it is his will.
He is the future of time, it is his choice.
Rome lives or dies by him; his heart,
His complex heart, decides the day or night!"
So speaks in ecstasy the Stagirite.
"It is his freedom, there rests all to come;
It is his self-creating will which rules,
But what he chooses—look! his mother's hand
Gave it him, look! look! he chooses her!"

For now the scene becomes hysterical
—"O now," the Marxian cries, "she would profess
That she is Rome, she would prevail by painting
Rome as her own face,
                          and one cannot
Discriminate Volumnia and Rome
In any sentence."
                    "O Marcius, Marcius,
Reconcile communities; be famous for
Your pity and your ruth,"
                          her foreign words
("She is convinced, she knows," Karl Marx affirms)
But he not yet convicted,
                          though she cries out,
"I am the hen that clucked you to the war,
I made you what you are, and no man, none,
Owes mother what you owe me."
                              Again they kneel,
Commanded by Volumnia.
                          He will not yield,
Although excruciated.
                          He will not yield,
He turns his face away,

Until she says, despairing, "Come,
Come wife, come child, this stranger's mother
Must be a Volscian. Come, he is no Roman,
He is no son, no husband and no father."

His knees slip under him, his weakness shows.
He cries out loudly, "Mother, Mother, Mother!
You win! God turns his face from us, appalled!
You win Rome's victory today,
                              but for your son,
You bring all danger on him, if not death,
You succor Rome but not your only son."

Soon he dismisses them with promised peace.
He will not go with them, no, he will stay,
An immigrant at Antium.
                              He asks
Aufidius, if he, Aufidius,
Could answer differently a mother
Or grant her less than he.
                              Aufidius
Pretends content,
                    aside vows Marcius' death,
Grateful for this excuse, new turncoat shift.

While Marcius courteously escorts
Mother and wife and child to carriages
To bring them back to Rome with happiness,
Congratulates them on their victory,
And turns to find how he must show himself
In the fresh disorder which his heart has made.

The scene in Rome. No hope or little hope
Abides.
          "Displace," Menenius cites, "displace
The capital with your little finger, then
Your hope is justified."
                              Displaced!

A newsboy means, the capital has been
Displaced! Volumnia's little finger did it!
She has prevailed with him and Rome is saved!
Joy is insane!
    Volumnia returns
And she is named the breathing life of Rome.

"She is, she is!" announces Sigmund Freud,
"All issue from the womb and must return;
The dandled, wiped and powdered babe
Cannot forget and cannot understand."
"Nature is no machine," says Aristotle,
"But like a whore she spreads herself, and man
Can do there what he wishes, all extremes."

"Who is that silent one?" I asked in fear,
"Who is that ghost who has not said one word?
Will he speak out before this play is done,
Take off his mask and show? He gives me dread,
You are my friends, you tell me all you know
—Though my stupidity distort it all—
Tell me his name now,
      free me from my fear!"
None answer, all intent, *katharsis* near!

For now the last scene shows: in Antium
Aufidius conspires. The Volscians are
Indeterminate as to the blunted war,
But hardly holding him at fault in it.
The city's lords convene. Marcius presents
All possible apology to them.
Points to the prizes won by him, Rome's shame,
The prosperous treaty made——
       "Traitor! Traitor!"
Aufidius calls out. The murderers
Close in on Marcius,
    who, merely amazed,
Is not yet angered.

"Marcius! Traitor!
Maudlin and pusillanimous!"
Aufidius reiterates,
                    Marcius explodes!
The insult lights his wrath.
                         "You lie!" he answers,
"You boy!" Aufidius calls back. "You boy!"
Though some would temporize, be moderate,
Marcius by this is overwhelmed:
                              "A boy!
A boy!" he howls, appalled, "Marcius!
Coriolanus in Corioli,
That is the name I took with my own hands."
(All tact is overthrown.)
                         "I cut my name
Into your soldiers' hearts, I, I, I,
Alone I did it! Boy!"
                    Aufidius
Grasps his permission here,
                           though one lord calls
For mercy to the boy,
                    Aufidius
Summons his fellows,
                    Marcius draws his sword,
They leap at him. *Kill! Kill! Kill!*
His heart is pierced.
                    Aufidius stands on him,
And thus the exhausted hero is struck down.
"And thus the exhausted hero is struck down,"
Says Aristotle, as the curtain falls,
"Even in the affirmation of himself."
"Acting the part which brought him to this pass,"
Marx chimes, with pity in his angry voice,
"True to himself amid so many truths."
"His choice, his wish, his heart, such is his fate,
All, all depends on the self-squeezing heart,"
Thus Aristotle adds, "Man's will is free,
This man became the man he chose to be!"

My face is covered by my hands to hide
Intolerable emotion, distorted look.

"Who is that man with you, O who is he?"
I questioned them as they began to fade,
"Who is the white masked one who said no word?"

"He is the one who saw what you did not!
He is the one who heard what you did not,"
So called the Stagirite, faint and unclear,
"He is the one you do not know, my dear."

II

Summer
Knowledge

4

THE
FULFILLMENT

At a Solemn Musick

Let the musicians begin,
Let every instrument awaken and instruct us
In love's willing river and love's dear discipline:
We wait, silent, in consent and in the penance
Of patience, awaiting the serene exaltation
Which is the liberation and conclusion of expiation.

Now may the chief musician say:
"Lust and emulation have dwelt among us
Like barbarous kings: have conquered us:
Have inhabited our hearts: devoured and ravished
—With the savage greed and avarice of fire—
The substance of pity and compassion."

Now may all the players play:
"The river of the morning, the morning of the river
Flow out of the splendor of the tenderness of surrender."

Now may the chief musician say:
"Nothing is more important than summer."

And now the entire choir shall chant:
"How often the astonished heart,
Beholding the laurel,
Remembers the dead,
And the enchanted absolute,
Snow's kingdom, sleep's dominion."

Then shall the chief musician declare:
"The phoenix is the meaning of the fruit,
Until the dream is knowledge and knowledge is a dream."

And then, once again, the entire choir shall cry, in passionate unity,
Singing and celebrating love and love's victory,

Ascending and descending the heights of assent, climbing and chant-
  ing triumphantly:
Before the morning was, you were:
Before the snow shone,
And the light sang, and the stone,
Abiding, rode the fullness or endured the emptiness,
You were: you were alone.

Darkling Summer, Ominous Dusk, Rumorous Rain

1

A tattering of rain and then the reign
Of pour and pouring-down and down,
Where in the westward gathered the filming gown
Of grey and clouding weakness, and, in the mane
Of the light's glory and the day's splendor, gold and vain,
Vivid, more and more vivid, scarlet, lucid and more luminous,
Then came a splatter, a prattle, a blowing rain!
And soon the hour was musical and rumorous:
A softness of a dripping lipped the isolated houses,
A gaunt grey somber softness licked the glass of hours.

2

Again, after a catbird squeaked in the special silence,
And clouding vagueness fogged the windowpane
And gathered blackness and overcast, the mane
Of light's story and light's glory surrendered and ended
—A pebble—a ring—a ringing on the pane,
A blowing and a blowing in: tides of the blue and cold
Moods of the great blue bay, and slates of grey
Came down upon the land's great sea, the body of this day
—Hardly an atom of silence amid the roar
Allowed the voice to form appeal—to call:
By kindled light we thought we saw the bronze of fall.

"Is it a dream?" I asked. To which my fellow
Answered with a hoarse voice and dulled insistence:
"Dream, is it a dream? What difference
Does it make or mean? If it is only a dream
It is the dream which we are. Dream or the last resort
Of reality, it is the truth of our minds:
We are condemned because this is our consciousness."

Where we were, if we were there, serene and shining
Each being sang and moved with the sleekness of rivers,
United in a choir, many and one, as the spires of flames in fire,
Flowing and perfected, flourishing and fulfilled forever,
Rising and falling as the carousel and palace of festival and victory.

"I was told often enough," my fellow said—
"You were told too—and you as little believed—
'Beware of all your desires. You are deceived.
(As they are deceived and deceptive, urgent and passing!)
They will be wholly fulfilled. You will be dead.
They will be gratified. And you will be dead!'"

In a fixed fascination, wonderstruck, we gazed,
Marveling at the fulfillment so long desired and praised.
There, effort was like dancing's its own pleasure.
There, all things existed purely in the action of joy—
Like light, like all kinds of light, all in the domination
      of celebration existed only as the structures of joy!

Then, as we gazed in an emotion more exhausting than mountains,
Then, when at last we knew where we had come,
It was then that we saw what was lost as we knew where we had been
(Or knew where we had been as we saw all that was lost!)
And knew for the first time the richness and poverty
Of what we had been before and were no more,

The striving, the suffering, the dear dark hooded mortality
Which we had been and never known, which we had resisted, detested,
feared and denied, the rocks and the flowers and the faces
of the needs and the hopes which had given us our reality!

The First Morning of the Second World

1

Suddenly.
Suddenly and certainly, as I watched elsewhere, locked
And intent in that vigil in which the hunter is hunted
As the mind is, seeking itself, falconer, falcon and hawk, victor and
victim,
Aware of the dry river beds, the droughts of the little deaths,
Sudden and overwhelming
Years rose and the damned waters of secret nature's underseas.
Where I had been before, tense and tired, was the edge of a winter
wood.
The gun of the mind ached in my numb and narrowed gaze,
Trembled a little, aimed at the pathless wood, and the snow-clouded
icewhite sky,
Hearing the rush not of the birds rising from bush and thicket thrash-
ing and clacking,
But suddenly the pouring continuous sibilance of waterfalls,
Certainly and suddenly, for a moment's eternity, it was the
        ecstasy and stillness of the white
        wizard blizzard, the white god fallen, united,
        entirely whiteness
The color of forgiveness, beginning and hope.

Quickly then and certainly it was the river of summer, blue as the
infinite curving blueness above us,
Little boats at anchor lolled or were lapped, and a yacht slowly glided.
It was wholly holiday, holiday absolute, a silk and saraband day, warm
and gay and
Blue and white and vibrant as the pennants buoyant on the stadium
near us,
White, a milk whiteness, and also all the colors flaring, melting, or
flowing.
There hope was, and the hopes, and the years past,

The beings I had known and forgotten and half-remembered or re-
membered too often,
Some in rowboats sunned, as on a picnic, or waiting, as before a play,
    the picnic and *the* play of eternity as summer, siesta, and summit
—How could I have known that the years and the hopes were human
    beings hated or loved,
Or known that I knew less and more than I supposed I supposed?
(So I questioned myself, in a voice familiar and strange.)
There they were, all of them, and I was with them,
They were with me, and they were me, I was them, forever united
As we all moved forward in a consonance silent and moving
        Seated and gazing,
            Upon the beautiful river forever.

2

So we were as children on the painted wooden horses, rising and fall-
    ing, of the carnival's carousel
Singing or smiling, at times, as the lyric of a small music tinkled
    above us
Saying: "The task is the round, the round is the task, the task and
    the round are a dance, and
There is nothing to think but drink of love and knowledge, and love's
    knowledge
When after and before are no more, and no more masks or un-
    masking,
        but only basking
(As the shining sea basks under the shining sun
In a radiance of swords and chandeliers dancing)
In the last love of knowledge, the first, when thought's abdication
    quickens thought's exaltation,
In the last blessing and sunlight of love's knowledge."

I hardly knew when my lips parted. Started to move slowly
As in the rehearsal of half-remembered memorized
        anthem, prayer, or spell
        of heartwelling gratitude and recognition.

My lips trembled, fumbled, and in the depths and death of thought
A murmur rose like the hidden humming of summer, when June
sleeps
In the radiant entrancings of warm light and green security.
Fumbling, feeling for what I had long supposed I had grasped and
cast aside as worthless,
the sparks or glitters of pleasure, trivial and transient.

—The phrases like faces came, lucid and vivid, separate, united, sin-
cere as pain
With the unity of meaning and emotion long lost, disbelieved or
denied,
As I sought with the words I had known a candid translation.
So I said then, in a language intimate and half-understood:
"I did not know . . . and I knew . . . surely I once knew . . .
I must have known . . .
Surely sometimes guessed at or suspected,
Knew and did not know what love is,
The measure of pleasure, heart of joy, the light and the heart of the
light
Which makes all pleasure, joy and love come to be
As light alone gives all colors being, the measure and the treasure
Of the light which unites and distinguishes the bondage and freedom
in unity and distinction
Which is love . . . Love? . . . Is love? What is love?"

Suddenly and certainly I saw how surely the measure and treasure of
pleasure is being as being with, belonging
Figured and touched in the experience of voices in chorus.
Withness is ripeness,
Ripeness is withness,
To be is to be in love,
Love is the fullness of being.

3

For the gratification of action by those who enact it and at once
In the enacting behold it, actual and antiphonal, *as* antiphonal in

154

another and others who are with them and look to them, toiling
and smiling,
Know the act and their enaction and another's and others' who suffer
the struggling,
The effort of effort, as in the toil and ecstasy of dancing and climbing,
When they know immediately within them what they see immedi-
ately without them, vivid in the faces, lucid in the voices,
Each creating and increasing the other, as fire in fire,
And as the lover knows *yes*, knows loving and being loved, *then*,
Kissing as he is kissed: then only effort is gratitude, then toil is
ecstasy,
Suffering is satisfaction and both are neither but a third,
Beyond and containing the fear and the striving, the excitement and
the rapture:
The self is another but with and wholly the self, loving and beloved;
Is neither no more and both, passing from both beyond to the being
of being
Self-hooded selfhood seeks in the darkness and daylight blind and
lost.

Suddenly, suddenly and certainly
Then it was as waking in the waters of morning, in winter,
Certainly it was the first morning again,
Waking in the first morning to a world outside of whiteness united,
Transfigured, possessed by the blessedness of whiteness and light,
A whiteness which was light and which was more than light,
And the inner morning and meaning of all light.

Suddenly it was the awe and moment when Adam first looked upon
another self, a self like his own self, yet an absolute other and new-
ness, being the beginning of being and love and loving and being
loved
(Then all astonishment rippled to recognition, unbelievable,
Yet actual before him, growing with the certainty, serenity and majesty
of morning).

Quickly and certainly it was the little moment when Lazarus
Thrusting aside the cold sweated linens,

Summoned by Jesus, snow and morning,
Thrust the stone to the side, the fell conclusion,
And knew all astonishment for the first time, wonderstruck
Not that he lived again, after the wood, the stone, the closing, nails,
and black silence empty,
But that he had ever died. Knew the illusion of death confused with
the reality of the agony of dying,
Knowing at last that death is inconceivable among the living
(Knowing the wish, the hope, the will, the luxury and ignorance of
the thought that man can ever die)
Hearing the thunder of the news of waking from the false dream of
life that life can ever end.

Summer Knowledge

Summer knowledge is not the winter's truth, the truth of fall,
  the autumn's fruition, vision, and recognition:
It is not May knowledge, little and leafing and growing green,
  blooming out and blossoming white,
It is not the knowing and the knowledge of the gold fall and
  the ripened darkening vineyard,
Nor the black tormented, drenched and rainy knowledge of birth,
  April, and travail,
The knowledge of the womb's convulsions, and the coiled cord's
  ravelled artery, severed and cut open,
  as the root forces its way up from the dark loam:
The agony of the first knowledge of pain is worse than death,
  or worse than the thought of death:
No poppy, no preparation, no initiation, no illusion, only
  the beginning, so distant from all knowledge
  and all conclusion, all indecision and all illusion.
Summer knowledge is green knowledge, country knowledge,
  the knowledge of growing and the supple recognition
  of the fullness and the fatness and the roundness of ripeness.
It is bird knowledge and the knowing that trees possess when
The sap ascends to the leaf and the flower and the fruit,
Which the root never sees and the root believes in the darkness
  and the ignorance of winter knowledge
—The knowledge of the fruit is not the knowledge possessed
  by the root in its indomitable darkness of ambition
Which is the condition of belief beyond conception of
  experience or the gratification of fruition.
Summer knowledge is not picture knowledge, nor is it the
  knowledge of lore and learning.
It is not the knowledge known from the mountain's height, it
  is not the garden's view of the distant mountains of hidden
    fountains;
It is not the still vision in a gold frame, it is not the
  measured and treasured sentences of sentiments;

It is cat knowledge, deer knowledge, the knowledge of the
    full-grown foliage, of the snowy blossom and the rounding fruit.
It is the phoenix knowledge of the vine and the grape near
    summer's end, when the grape swells and the apple reddens:
It is the knowledge of the ripening apple when it moves to the
    fullness of the time of falling to rottenness and death.
For summer knowledge is the knowledge of death as birth,
Of death as the soil of all abounding flowering flaring rebirth.
It is the knowledge of the truth of love and the truth of growing:
    it is the knowledge before and after knowledge:
For, in a way, summer knowledge is not knowledge at all: it is
    second nature, first nature fulfilled, a new birth
    and a new death for rebirth, soaring and rising out
    of the flames of turning October, burning November,
    the towering and falling fires, growing more and
    more vivid and tall
In the consummation and the annihilation of the blaze of fall.

5

MORNING BELLS

"I Am Cherry Alive," the Little Girl Sang

For Miss Kathleen Hanlon

"I am cherry alive," the little girl sang,
"Each morning I am something new:
I am apple, I am plum, I am just as excited
As the boys who made the Hallowe'en bang:
I am tree, I am cat, I am blossom too:
When I like, if I like, I can be someone new,
Someone very old, a witch in a zoo:
I can be someone else whenever I think who,
And I want to be everything sometimes too:
And the peach has a pit and I know that too,
And I put it in along with everything
To make the grown-ups laugh whenever I sing:
And I sing: *It is true; It is untrue;*
I know, I know, the true is untrue,
The peach has a pit, the pit has a peach:
And both may be wrong when I sing my song,
But I don't tell the grown-ups: because it is sad,
And I want them to laugh just like I do
Because they grew up and forgot what they knew
And they are sure I will forget it some day too.
They are wrong. They are wrong. When I sang my song, I knew, I
   knew!
I am red, I am gold, I am green, I am blue,
I will always be me, I will always be new!"

O child, when you go down to sleep and sleep's secession,
You become more and other than you are, you become
       the procession
Of bird and beast and tree: you are a chorus,
A pony among horses, a sapling in a dark forest,
Lifting your limbs and boughs to the sky, leafing.
And then you are one with the beaver, one
With the little animals warm in the sun
Resting and hidden when it is white winter:
       And in sleep's river you sleep
       Like the river's self and the marine
       Beings who mouth as they glide, nosing
         And sliding lithely and smoothly
           Gleaming serenely and sleekly.

Jeremiah Dickson was a true-blue American,
For he was a little boy who understood America, for he felt that he
   must
Think about *everything*; because that's *all* there is to think about,
Knowing immediately the intimacy of truth and comedy,
Knowing intuitively how a sense of humor was a necessity
For one and for all who live in America. Thus, natively, and
Naturally when on an April Sunday in an ice cream parlor Jeremiah
Was requested to choose between a chocolate sundae and a banana
   split
He answered unhesitatingly, having no need to think of it
Being a true-blue American, determined to continue as he began:
Rejecting the either-or of Kierkegaard, and many another European;
Refusing to accept alternatives, refusing to believe the choice of
   between;
Rejecting selection; denying dilemma; electing absolute affirmation:
   knowing
      in his breast
         The infinite and the gold
         Of the endless frontier, the deathless West.

"Both: I will have them both!" declared this true-blue American
In Cambridge, Massachusetts, on an April Sunday, instructed
      By the great department stores, by the Five-and-Ten,
Taught by Christmas, by the circus, by the vulgarity and grandeur of
      Niagara Falls and the Grand Canyon,
Tutored by the grandeur, vulgarity, and infinite appetite gratified and
      Shining in the darkness, of the light
On Saturdays at the double bills of the moon pictures,
The consummation of the advertisements of the imagination of the
   light
Which is as it was—the infinite belief in infinite hope—of Columbus,
   Barnum, Edison, and Jeremiah Dickson.

Come, let us meditate upon the fate of a little boy who wished to be
Hungarian! Having been moved with his family to a new suburb,
  having been sent to a new school, the only Catholic school in the
  new suburb,
Where all the other children were Hungarian,

He felt very sad and separate on the first day, he felt more and more
  separated and isolated
Because all the other boys and girls pitied and were sorry for him
  since he was not
Hungarian! Hence they pitied and were sorry for him so much they
  gave him handsome gifts,
Presents of comic books, marbles and foreign coins, peppermints and
  candy, a pistol, and also their devoted sympathy, pity and friendship

Making him sadder still since now he saw how all Hungarians were
  very kind and generous, and he was not

Hungarian! Hence he was an immigrant, an alien: he was and he
  would be,
Forever, no matter what, he could never become Hungarian!
Hungarian! Hence he went home on the first day, bearing his gifts
  and telling his parents how much he wished to be
Hungarian: in anguish, in anger,
Accusing them of depriving him, and misusing him: amusing them,
So that he rose to higher fury, shouting and accusing them

—Because of you I am a stranger, monster, orang-outang!
Because of you (his hot tears say) I am an orang-outang! and not
Hungarian! Worse than to have no bicycle, no shoes . . .
        Behold how this poor boy, who wished so passionately to be
        Hungarian
        Suffered and knew the fate of being American.
            Whether on Ellis Island, Plymouth Rock,

Or in the secret places of the mind and heart
This is America—as poetry and hope
This is the fame, the game and the names of our fate:
This we must suffer or must celebrate.

Is It the Morning? Is It the Little Morning?

Is it morning? Is it the little morning
Just before dawn? How big the sun is!
Are those the birds? Their voices begin
Everywhere, whistling, piercing, and joyous
All over and in the air, speaking the words
Which are more than words, with mounting consciousness:
And everything begins to rise to the brightening
Of the slow light that ascends to the blaze's lightning!

A *Small Score*

Meek, sang the crickets, wheat, meet, creek,
And the birds sang *tutti*, all of them:
    "Bubble, little,
    Whistle, pretty,
    Trickle, whittle,
    Lipping and dripping
    Sipping the well
    Where the fawn dipped
    Before dawn descended
    And darkness surrendered
    To the rising of the sovereign splendor,
    The great bell and ball
    Of supreme abundance and blazing radiance."
Thus, thus, the little birds sang in charming disorder and full chorus
To greet gravely, sweetly and most meetly
The blaze of majesty soaring in great oars,
And their twinkling and carolling grew more and more
      sure as they saw the great roar of awe
        arising surely all over the great blue
          bay above them.

A *Little Morning Music*

The birds in the first light twitter and whistle,
Chirp and seek, sipping and chortling—weakly, meekly, they speak
and bubble
As cheerful as the cherry would, if it could speak when it is cherry
ripe or cherry ripening.
And all of them are melodious, erratic, and gratuitous,
Singing solely to heighten the sense of morning's beginning.
How soon the heart's cup overflows, how it is excited to delight and
elation!

And in the first light, the cock's chant, roaring,
Bursts like rockets, rising and breaking into brief brilliance;
As the fields arise, cock after cock catches on fire,
And the pastures loom out of vague blue shadow,
The red barn and the red sheds rise and redden, blocks and boxes
of slowly blooming wet redness;
Then the great awe and splendor of the sun comes nearer,
Kindling all things, consuming the forest of blackness, lifting and light-
ing up
All the darkling ones who slept and grew
Beneath the petals, the frost, the mystery and the mockery of the
stars.
The darkened ones turn slightly in the faint light of the small morning,
Grow grey or glow green—
They are grey or green at once
        In the pale cool of blue light;
They dream of that other life and that otherness
Which is the darkness, going over
Maple and oak, leafy and rooted in the ancient and famous light,
In the bondage of the soil of the past and the radiance of the future.
But now the morning is growing, the sun is soaring, all
That lights up shows, quickly or slowly, the showing plenitude of
fountains,
And soon an overflowing radiance, actual and dazzling, will blaze and
brim over all of us,

Discovering and uncovering all color and all kinds, all forms and all
distances, rising and rising higher
    and higher, like a stupendous bonfire of consciousness,
Gazing and blazing, blessing and possessing all vividness and all
darkness.

6

THE
KINGDOM
OF
POETRY

Gold Morning, Sweet Prince

What the sad and passionate gay player of Avon avowed
With vivid exactness, eloquent variety is, as immense
As the sea is. The sea which neither the humble nor the proud
Can dam, control or master. No matter what our sense
Of existence, or whence we come or where we hope and seek
He knew us all before we were, he knew the strong, the weak,
The silly, the reticent, the pious, the powerful, the experience
Of fortune, sudden fame, extremes reversed, inevitable loss
Whether on land or sea. He knew mortality's immortality
And essential uncertainty, as he knew the land and sea.

He knew the reality of nobility.
He saw the cowering, towering power of treachery.
He hated the flakes and butterflies of lechery.
And he believed, at times, in truth, hope, loyalty and charity.

See: he saw what was and what is and what has yet to come to be:
A gentle monarch murdered in helpless sleep.
A girl by Regent Hypocrisy seduced.
A child by Archduke Ambition stabbed and killed.
A loving loyal wife by a husband loyal and brave,
Falsely suspected, by a handkerchief accused,
Stabbed by his love, his innocence, his trust
In the glib cleverness of a self-hating knave.

Look: Ophelia lolls and babbles in the river named Forever,
Never Never Never Never Never.
Cordelia is out of breath and Lear
Has learned at last that flattery is clever
That words are free, sentiments inexpensive, vows
And declarations worthless and priceless: at last he knows
How true love is sometimes speechless, always sincere.
He knows—and knows too late—that love was very near and dear.

Are all hearts and all girls always betrayed?
Is love never beyond lust, disgust, and distrust?
See: it is clear: Duncan is in his grave,
While Desdemona weeps beneath the willow tree,
Having been granted little time to weep, pray or rave:
Is this the truth, the truth which is one, eternal, and whole?
Surely the noble, the innocent, the gifted and the brave
Sometimes—surely, at times—prevail. Yet if one living soul
Is caught by cruelty and killed by trust
Whence is our consolation above or before the grave?

Ripeness is all: the rest is silence. Love
Is all; we are such stuff as love has made us
And our little life, green, ripe, or rotten, is what it is
Because of love accepted, rejected, refused and jilted, faded, raided,
    neglected or betrayed.
Some are defeated, some are mistreated, some are fulfilled, some come
    to flower and succeed
In knowing the patience of energy from the dark root to the rounding
    fruit.
And if this were not true, if love were not kind and cruel,
Generous and unjust, heartless and irresistible, painful to the savant
    and gentle to the fool,
Fecund and various, wasteful and precarious, lavish, savage, greedy
    and tender, begetting the lion and the lamb
The peacock, the spaniel, the tiger, the lizard, the chicken hawk and
    the dove,
All would be nothing much, all would be trivial, nothing would be
    enough, love would not be love.
For, as there is no game and no victory when no one loses
So there is no choice but the choice of love, unless one chooses
Never to love, seeking immunity, discovering nothingness.

This is the only sanctuary, this is the one asylum unless
We hide in a dark ark, and deny, refuse to believe in hope's con-
    sciousness,
Deny hope's reality, until hope descends, in the unknown, hidden and
    ultimate love,

174

Crying forever with all the others who are damned and hopeless that
 love is not love.

Gold morning, sweet prince, black night has always descended and
 has always ended,
Gold morning, prince of Avon, sovereign and king
Of reality, hope, and speech, may all the angels sing
With all the sweetness and all the truth with which you sang of any-
 thing and everything.

VIVALDI

e vo significando

Music consists of men in black and red climbing a broad staircase. GOETHE

Withness is all

In the dark church of music
    Which never is of land or sea alone
But blooms within the air inside the mind,
Patterns in motion and in action, successions
Of processionals, moving with the majesty of certainty
To part the unparted curtains, to bring the chandeliers
Allegro Into the saraband of courtiers who have bowed and curtsied,
con Turned somersaults in circuses, climbed masts and towers,
molto Or dived as from a glittering tower toward a glistening lake
Diving daring and assured, fearless and precise
                    to find in the darkness the dark church

Which music is: this is what music is
It has no meaning and is possessed by all meaning,
For music says:
        Remorse, here is the scar of healing,
        Here is a window, curiosity!
        And here, O sensuality, a sofa!
        Behold, for ambition's purposeless energy
        Mountains rising beyond the mountains
        More tense and steep than any known before

2

Devout
The processional (having a solemn majesty
Andante Though childlike acrobats like flowers decorate

176

With flourishes and *entrechats* the passage to success
As queens serene crowned by poise, slowly
Are drawn in cars by dragons domesticated in the last of wars.)
Is uttered fully and yet freshly, newly and uniquely.
Uniquely and newly, freshly yet fully repeated then.

3

O clear soprano like the morning peal of the bluebells,
Scherzo   O the watercolors of the early morning,
con amore and *vivace!* dancing, prancing, galloping, rollicking!

This is the surrender to the splendor of being's becoming and being!
Allegro   Here are all the flowers and the images of faces as flowers of fear and
cantabile   hope, longing and despair,
Here is the hour of the new blue flower
. . . Dissolved, consumed in this being which is the being of being,
So we are to be contained, so we are to be consumed
The iron flower of the flute possesses morning's intuition,
The cellist is as Gautama Buddha, curved like an almond,
Noah conducts the ark of all the dark beauty,
The first violinist is Assisi's Francis,
                blessing the trees, the cats, the birds,
                        calling to them, his brothers and his
                                sisters
The full orchestra responds to the virtuoso's cadenza:
"Love is the dark secret of everything
Love is the open secret of everything,
An open secret useless as the blue!"

Music is not water, but it moves like water,
It is not fire, but it soars as warm as the sun.
It is not rock, it is not fountain,
                But rock and fountain, clock and mountain
Abide within it, bound together,
In radiance pulsing vibrating and reverberating,
Dominating the domination of the weather!

The music flowing as a river and a city

Adagio   and a city ringed about a river

con   and a river mastered by a city

molto   Has destiny's look; the dictates of the heart

And the heart's dictatorship must submit

To the score of the lyre gentled like all fire

To ashen falling failure. The music, although unseen,

Is hushed nor more nor less than snow's fall, slowly falling,

After being possessed by the dynasty of destiny

and then,

     and then,

Allegro   Is suddenly more selfdelighting than a troop of birds in swinging sing-

vivace   ing ringing curving flights

In curves and swerves, dipping and perching, perching and soaring,

    sailing.

The music declares:

Coda   "Is this what you want? Is this the goodness for which you have been

    here convened?

"To be, to become, and to participate in the sweet congress of serene

    attention?"

Silent, attentive, motionless, waiting,

     Save for the heart clutching itself and the hushed breathing

(A sudden cough!) sticks-in the enchantment's dancing,

The answered question is: Our being. Our presence. Our surrender.

Consciousness has consented, is consumed, has surrendered, to hear

    only the players playing:

Consciousness has become only and purely listening,

    The vivid world has been barred,

    The press of desire shut out

    All lights are dim save for this swan, unseen

    The port and ark of Panurge, sailing the darkness

    All desire consumed except the desire of this being,

    The presence of this being, the being of this presence,

    This present, this being: *this* is the being

The dream strives towards, and passion presses forward
   (Above the clouds and the shrouds,
   Rising like a plane forever)
   Far from the world of Caesar and Venus, calculation and sensuality,
      ratiocination and frustration,
This is the dark city of the hidden innermost wish,
   The motion beyond emotion,
      The power beyond and free of power,
         Beyond beyond within the withness of witness,
This is the immortality of mortality, this
Is supreme consciousness,
The self-forgetting in the self possessed and mastered
   In the elation of being open to all relation
No longer watchful, wakeful, guarded, wary, no longer striving and
   climbing:
This is the immortality of immortality
      Deathless and present in the presence of the deathless present.
This is the grasped reality of reality, moving forward
      Now and forever.

Sterne

To *Gloria Macdonald*

Held on bondage day and night
By dear my Lord Fauconberg. With whom I dined
At the Boar's Head. There the whole Pandemonium,
Assembled, supped. Have just been eating chicken, weeping,
Seated and weeping, the tears fall over it,
A bitter sauce.

I have doubled the Cape of Good Hope.
I have looked in Yorick's face.

I wish I were in Arno's vale,
Though here at Coxwold, days are princely
—A land of plenty, and I dine
On trout, on venison, and on wild fowl.

Yet as I eat my strawberries, for want of you
I am as melancholy as a cat. I have a cat now.
Sits beside me, quietly and gravely purrs
To my sorrows, gazes at me solemnly
As if he knew the reason of my pain!

—How soothable the heart is, dear Eliza!
Supported when it sinks pathetically
By a poor beast purring harmoniously!
When a poor cat purrs *pianissimo*
Me, me, poor Yorick harks to an anodyne
Dark and sweet as the poppy, fresh and rash as the cock's cocorico!

. . . Love, alas, has fled with thee
Whom all the night my wakeful eyes
(While all the day is blind to me!)
Imagine, summon, idolize
Standing before dim gates, or pitifully
(Such is my hope, my vanity!)
Waiting in the great green park most patiently!

Swift

What shall Presto do for pretty prattle
To entertain his dears? Sunday: lightning fifty times!
This week to Flanders goes the Duke of Ormond!
Shall hope of him, although he loves me well!

All of my hopes now possible,
None certain. As, my lampoon
Talked up all over, cried up to the sky
—You are an impudent slut to be so positive
Though all has gone just as you said it would!
Sirrah! write constantly! don't I write every day
And sometimes twice? Stella writes like an emperor.

Sirrah, I am surprised forever—by myself!
Or by the others—dee dee: an angel child
Stupid in me, stupid or innocent
Astonished by the gush of vanity
The stone and eyes of pride—yet equally
By the least straw or glitter of nobility!
—Faith, Madame Dingley, what think you of the world to come?
Patience! Patience is a gay thing—O saucy rogues,
Patience is better than knowledge: be gay till I return.

Mr. Harley speaks every kind thing to me.
Truly, I do believe, would serve me if I stayed
—Called at the coffee house, stayed there a while,
Coldly conversed with Mr. Addison:

All our friendship and dearness now are off:
Is it not odd? I think he has used me ill:
I have as little pleasure as anyone
In all the world, although I am
In full favor with the entire ministry.

Nothing gives Presto any dream of happiness
But letters now and then from his deelest ones.

The pride of power, the pride and pleasure of place and power are
    Towers
And trivial toys which lure me grievously
Ravaging furiously in a lunation's infuriation . . .
Bursting the Rome in my head, my empire!
Gulliver? Gullible! The Caesars in my heart
Tell me how all infamy is possible,
And certain treacheries extremely probable!

I must take leave of deelest MD now. Prithee,
Be merry, patient girls and love your Presto.
I have read all the trash and I am weary:
Deelest lives, there is peace and quiet with thee
And thee alone. None have the leisure here for little things.
Farewell again, dear rogues; I am never happy
But when I think of thee MD. Sirrah,
I have had enough of courts and ministries.
I wish I were once more at Laracor:
Faith, do you know each syllable I write
I hold my lips exact for all the world
As if I talked the little language with MD.

Yesterday died the Duke of Ormond's daughter:
Poor dear, she was with child. She was
My favourite pet—save thee—I hardly knew
A being more valuable, more beautiful,
Of more nobility. I fear the certainty
That she was thrown away quite carelessly,
And merely lacked care. 'Tis clear, at any rate,
That she was very healthy naturally.
—Her Lord's a puppy. I'll no more of him,
Now that he's lost his only valuable . . .
—I hate life when I see it thus exposed
To accidents like these, so many thousands

Burthening the earth with their stupidity,
While such as she must die—abruptly—pointlessly.

Somebody is coming wants a little place.
My heart is set upon the cherry trees
By the river side. My saucy sluts
Farewell my deelest Nite poo dee MD . . .

Y'see a Sea that's ten miles wide, a town
On t'other side, ships sailing in the Sea
Discharging great Canons at MDs and mee,
I see a great Sky, Moon and Stars, and ALL:
                        I am a Fool.

Hölderlin

Now as before do you not hear their voices
Serene in the midst of their rejoicing
Chanting to those who have hopes and make choices
Clear as the birds in the thick summer foliage:
                    It is! It is!
                    We are! We are!
Clearly, as if they were us, and not us,
Hidden like the future, distant as the stars,
Having no more meaning than the fullness of music,
Chanting from the pure peaks where success,
Effort and desire are meaningless,
Surpassed at last in the joy of joy,
Chanting at last the blue's last view:
                    It is! It is!
                    This is eternity! Eternity is now!

When I fall asleep, and even during sleep,
I hear, quite distinctly, voices speaking
Whole phrases, commonplace and trivial,
Having no relation to my affairs.

Dear Mother, is any time left to us
In which to be happy? My debts are immense.
My bank account is subject to the court's judgment.
I know nothing. I cannot know anything.
I have lost the ability to make an effort.
But now as before my love for you increases.
You are always armed to stone me, always:
It is true. It dates from childhood.

For the first time in my long life
I am almost happy. The book, almost finished,
Almost seems good. It will endure, a monument
To my obsessions, my hatred, my disgust.

Debts and inquietude persist and weaken me.
Satan glides before me, saying sweetly:
"Rest for a day! You can rest and play today.
Tonight you will work." When night comes,
My mind, terrified by the arrears,
Bored by sadness, paralyzed by impotence,
Promises: "Tomorrow: I will tomorrow."
Tomorrow the same comedy enacts itself
With the same resolution, the same weakness.

I am sick of this life of furnished rooms.
I am sick of having colds and headaches:
You know my strange life. Every day brings

Its quota of wrath. You little know
A poet's life, dear Mother: I must write poems,
The most fatiguing of occupations.

I am sad this morning. Do not reproach me.
I write from a café near the post office,
Amid the click of billiard balls, the clatter of dishes,
The pounding of my heart. I have been asked to write
"A History of Caricature." I have been asked to write
"A History of Sculpture." Shall I write a history
Of the caricatures of the sculptures of you in my heart?

Although it costs you countless agony,
Although you cannot believe it necessary,
And doubt that the sum is accurate,
Please send me money enough for at least three weeks.

The Kingdom of Poetry

This is like light.
This is light,
Useful as light, as charming and
as enchanting . . .

. . . Poetry is certainly
More interesting, more valuable,
and certainly more charming
Than Niagara Falls, the Grand Canyon, the Atlantic Ocean
And other much admired natural phenomena.
It is useful as light, and as beautiful.
It is preposterous
Precisely, making it possible to say
One cannot carry a mountain, but a poem can be carried all over.
It is monstrous
Pleasantly, for poetry can say, seriously or in play:

"Poetry is better than hope,
"For Poetry is the patience of hope, and all hope's vivid pictures,
"Poetry is better than excitement, it is far more delightful,
"Poetry is superior to success, and victory, it endures in serene
blessedness
"Long after the most fabulous feat like fireworks has mounted and
fallen.
"Poetry is a far more powerful and far more enchanting animal
"Than any wood, jungle, ark, circus or zoo possesses."

For Poetry magnifies and heightens reality:
Poetry says of reality that if it is magnificent, it is also stupid:
For poetry is, in a way, omnipotent;
For reality is various and rich, powerful and vivid, but it is not enough
Because it is disorderly and stupid or only at times, and erratically,
intelligent:
For without poetry, reality is speechless or incoherent:
It is inchoate, like the pomp and bombast of thunder:

187

Its perorations verge upon the ceaseless oration of the ocean:
For reality's glow and glory, without poetry,
Fade, like the red operas of sunset,
     The blue rivers and windows of morning.

The art of poetry makes it possible to say: *Pandemonium*.
     For poetry is gay and exact. It says:
     "The sunset resembles a bull-fight.
     "A sleeping arm feels like soda, fizzing."
Poetry resurrects the past from the sepulchre, like Lazarus.
It transforms a lion into a sphinx and a girl.
It gives to a girl the splendor of Latin.
It transforms the water into wine at each marriage in Cana of Galilee.
For it is true that poetry invented the unicorn, the centaur and the
     phoenix.
Hence it is true that poetry is an everlasting Ark,
An omnibus containing, bearing and begetting all the mind's animals.
Whence it is that poetry gave and gives tongue to forgiveness
Therefore a history of poetry would be a history of joy, and a history
     of the mystery of love
For poetry provides spontaneously, abundantly and freely
The petnames and the diminutives which love requires and without
     which the mystery of love cannot be mastered.

For poetry is like light, and it is light.
It shines over all, like the blue sky, with the same blue justice.
For poetry is the sunlight of consciousness:
It is also the soil of the fruits of knowledge
          In the orchards of being:
     It shows us the pleasures of the city.
     It lights up the structures of reality.
     It is a cause of knowledge and laughter:
     It sharpens the whistles of the witty:
     It is like morning and the flutes of morning, chanting and en-
          chanted.
     It is the birth and rebirth of the first morning forever.

Poetry is quick as tigers, clever as cats, vivid as oranges,
Nevertheless, it is deathless: it is evergreen and in blossom; long after
the Pharaohs and Caesars have fallen,
It shines and endures more than diamonds,
This is because poetry is the actuality of possibility. It is
The reality of the imagination,
The throat of exaltation,
The procession of possession,
The motion of meaning and
The meaning of morning and
The mastery of meaning.

The praise of poetry is like the clarity of the heights of the mountains.
The heights of poetry are like the exaltation of the mountains.
It is the consummation of consciousness in the country of the morning!

Seurat's Sunday Afternoon along the Seine

To Meyer and Lillian Schapiro

What are they looking at? Is it the river?
The sunlight on the river, the summer, leisure,
Or the luxury and nothingness of consciousness?
A little girl skips, a ring-tailed monkey hops
Like a kangaroo, held by a lady's lead
(Does the husband tax the Congo for the monkey's keep?)
The hopping monkey cannot follow the poodle dashing ahead.

Everyone holds his heart within his hands:

A prayer, a pledge of grace or gratitude
A devout offering to the god of summer, Sunday and plenitude.

The Sunday people are looking at hope itself.

They are looking at hope itself, under the sun, free from the teething
    anxiety, the gnawing nervousness
Which wastes so many days and years of consciousness.

The one who beholds them, beholding the gold and green
Of summer's Sunday is himself unseen. This is because he is
Dedicated radiance, supreme concentration, fanatically threading
The beads, needles and eyes—at once!—of vividness and permanence.
He is a saint of Sunday in the open air, a fanatic disciplined
By passion, courage, passion, skill, compassion, love: the love of life
    and the love of light as one, under the sun, with the love of life.

Everywhere radiance glows like a garden in stillness blossoming.

Many are looking, many are holding something or someone
Little or big: some hold several kinds of parasols:
Each one who holds an umbrella holds it differently

One hunches under his red umbrella as if he hid
And looked forth at the river secretly, or sought to be
Free of all of the others' judgement and proximity.
Next to him sits a lady who has turned to stone, or become a boulder,
Although her bell-and-sash hat is red.
A little girl holds to her mother's arm
As if it were a permanent genuine certainty:
Her broad-brimmed hat is blue and white, blue like the river, like the
    sailboats white,
And her face and her look have all the bland innocence,
Open and far from fear as cherubims playing harpsichords.
An adolescent girl holds a bouquet of flowers
As if she gazed and sought her unknown, hoped-for, dreaded destiny.
No hold is as strong as the strength with which the trees,
Grip the ground, curve up to the light, abide in the warm kind air:
Rooted and rising with a perfected tenacity
Beyond the distracted erratic case of mankind there.
Every umbrella curves and becomes a tree,
And the trees curving, arise to become and be
Like the umbrella, the bells of Sunday, summer, and Sunday's luxury.
Assured as the trees is the strolling dignity
Of the bourgeois wife who holds her husband's arm
With the easy confidence and pride of one who is
—She is sure—a sovereign Victorian empress and queen.
Her husband's dignity is as solid as his *embonpoint*:
He holds a good cigar, and a dainty cane, quite carelessly.
He is held by his wife, they are each other's property,
Dressed quietly and impeccably, they are suave and grave
As if they were unaware or free of time, and the grave,
Master and mistress of Sunday's promenade—of everything!
—As they are absolute monarchs of the ring-tailed monkey.
If you look long enough at anything
It will become extremely interesting;
If you look very long at anything
It will become rich, manifold, fascinating:

If you can look at any thing for long enough,
You will rejoice in the miracle of love,

You will possess and be blessed by the marvellous blinding radiance
   of love, you will be radiance.
Selfhood will possess and be possessed, as in the consecration of marriage, the mastery of vocation, the mystery of gift's mastery, the
   deathless relation of parenthood and progeny.
All things are fixed in one direction:
We move with the Sunday people from right to left.

The sun shines
In soft glory
Mankind finds
The famous story
Of peace and rest, released for a little while from the tides of weekday
   tiredness, the grinding anxiousness
Of daily weeklong lifelong fear and insecurity,
The profound nervousness which in the depths of consciousness
Gnaws at the roots of the teeth of being so continually, whether in
   sleep or wakefulness,
We are hardly aware that it is there or that we might ever be free
Of its ache and torment, free and open to all experience.

The Sunday summer sun shines equally and voluptuously
Upon the rich and the free, the comfortable, the *rentier*, the poor,
   and those who are paralyzed by poverty.
Seurat is at once painter, poet, architect, and alchemist:
The alchemist points his magical wand to describe and hold the Sun-
   day's gold,
Mixing his small alloys for long and long
Because he wants to hold the warm leisure and pleasure of the holiday
Within the fiery blaze and passionate patience of his gaze and mind
Now and forever: O happy, happy throng,
It is forever Sunday, summer, free: you are forever warm
Within his little seeds, his small black grains,
He builds and holds the power and the luxury
With which the summer Sunday serenely reigns.

—Is it possible? It is possible!—
Although it requires the labors of Hercules, Sisyphus, Flaubert,
   Roebling:

The brilliance and spontaneity of Mozart, the patience of a pyramid,
And requires all these of the painter who at twenty-five
Hardly suspects that in six years he will no longer be alive!
—His marvellous little marbles, beads, or molecules
Begin as points which the alchemy's magic transforms
Into diamonds of blossoming radiance, possessing and blessing the
visual:
For look how the sun shines anew and newly, transfixed
By his passionate obsession with serenity
As he transforms the sunlight into the substance of pewter, glittering,
poised and grave, vivid as butter,
In glowing solidity, changeless, a gift, lifted to immortality.

The sunlight, the soaring trees and the Seine
Are as a great net in which Seurat seeks to seize and hold
All living being in a parade and promenade of mild, calm happiness:
The river, quivering, silver blue under the light's variety,
Is almost motionless. Most of the Sunday people
Are like flowers, walking, moving toward the river, the sun, and the
river of the sun.
Each one holds some thing or some one, some instrument
Holds, grasps, grips, clutches or somehow touches
Some form of being as if the hand and fist of holding and possessing,
Alone and privately and intimately, were the only genuine lock or
bond of blessing.

A young man blows his flute, curved by pleasure's musical activity,
His back turned upon the Seine, the sunlight, and the sunflower day.
A dapper dandy in a top hat gazes idly at the Seine:
The casual delicacy with which he holds his cane
Resembles his tailored elegance.
He sits with well-bred posture, sleek and pressed,
Fixed in his niche: he is his own mustache.
A working man slouches parallel to him, quite comfortable,
Lounging or lolling, leaning on his elbow, smoking a meerschaum,
Gazing in solitude, at ease and oblivious or contemptuous
Although he is very near the elegant young gentleman.
Behind him a black hound snuffles the green, blue ground.

Between them, a wife looks down upon
The knitting in her lap, as in profound
Scrutiny of a difficult book. For her constricted look
Is not in her almost hidden face, but in her holding hands
Which hold the knitted thing as no one holds
Umbrella, kite, sail, flute or parasol.

This is the nervous reality of time and time's fire which turns
Whatever is into another thing, continually altering and changing all
    identity, as time's great fire burns (aspiring, flying and dying),
So that all things arise and fall, living, leaping and fading, falling, like
    flames aspiring, flowering, flying and dying—
Within the uncontrollable blaze of time and of history:
Hence Seurat seeks within the cave of his gaze and mind to find
A permanent monument to Sunday's simple delight; seeks deathless
    joy through the eye's immortality;
Strives patiently and passionately to surpass the fickle erratic quality
    of living reality.

Within this Sunday afternoon upon the Seine
Many pictures exist inside the Sunday scene:
Each of them is a world itself, a world in itself (and as a living child
    links generations, reconciles the estranged and aged so that a grand-
    child is a second birth, and the rebirth of the irrational, of those
    who are forlorn, resigned or implacable),
Each little picture links the large and small, grouping the big
Objects, connecting them with each little dot, seed or black grain
Which are as patterns, a marvellous network and tapestry,
Yet have, as well, the random freshness and radiance
Of the rippling river's sparkle, the frost's astonishing systems,
As they appear to morning's waking, a pure, white delicate stillness
    and minuet,
In December, in the morning, white pennants streaked upon the
    windowpane.

He is fanatical: he is at once poet and architect,
Seeking complete evocation in forms as strong as the Eiffel Tower,

Subtle and delicate too as one who played a Mozart sonata, alone,
  under the spires of Notre-Dame.
Quick and utterly sensitive, purely real and practical,
Making a mosaic of the little dots into a mural of the splendor of
  order:
Each micro pattern is the dreamed of or imagined macrocosmos
In which all things, big and small, in willingness and love surrender
To the peace and elation of Sunday light and sunlight's pleasure, to
  the profound measure and order of proportion and relation.

He reaches beyond the glistening spontaneity
Of the dazzled Impressionists who follow
The changing light as it ranges, changing, moment by moment, ar-
  ranging and charming and freely bestowing
All freshness and all renewal continually on all that shows and flows.

Although he is very careful, he is entirely candid.
Although he is wholly impersonal, he has youth's frankness and, such
  is his candor,
His gaze is unique and thus it is intensely personal:
It is never facile, glib, or mechanical,
His vision is simple: yet it is also ample, complex, vexed, and profound
In emulation of the fullness of Nature maturing and enduring and
  toiling with the chaos of actuality.

An infinite variety within a simple frame:
Countless variations upon a single theme!
Vibrant with what soft soft luster, what calm joy!
This is the celebration of contemplation,
This is the conversion of experience to pure attention,
Here is the holiness of all the little things
Offered to us, discovered for us, transformed into the vividest con-
  sciousness,
After the shallowness or blindness of experience,
After the blurring, dirtying sooted surfaces which, since Eden and
  since birth,
Make all the little things trivial or unseen,
Or tickets quickly torn and thrown away

En route by rail to an ever-receding holiday:
—Here we have stopped, here we have given our hearts
To the real city, the vivid city, the city in which we dwell
And which we ignore or disregard most of the luminous day!

. . . Time passes: nothing changes, everything stays the same. Noth-
  ing is new
Under the sun. It is also true
That time passes and everything changes, year by year, day by day,
Hour by hour. Seurat's *Sunday Afternoon along the Seine* has gone
  away,
Has gone to Chicago: near Lake Michigan,
All of his flowers shine in monumental stillness fulfilled.
And yet it abides elsewhere and everywhere where images
Delight the eye and heart, and become the desirable, the admirable,
  the willed
Icons of purified consciousness. Far and near, close and far away
Can we not hear, if we but listen to what Flaubert tried to say,
Beholding a husband, wife and child on just such a day:
Ils sont dans le vrai! They are with the truth, they have found the way
The kingdom of heaven on earth on Sunday summer day.
Is it not clear and clearer? Can we not also hear
The voice of Kafka, forever sad, in despair's sickness trying to say:
"Flaubert was right: *Ils sont dans le vrai!*
Without forbears, without marriage, without heirs,
Yet with a wild longing for forbears, marriage, and heirs:
They all stretch out their hands to me: but they are too far away!"

7

THE
DECEPTIVE
PRESENT,
THE
PHOENIX YEAR

The world was warm and white when I was born:
Beyond the windowpane the world was white,
A glaring whiteness in a leaded frame,
Yet warm as in the hearth and heart of light.
Although the whiteness was almond and was bone
In midnight's still paralysis, nevertheless
The world was warm and hope was infinite
All things would come, fulfilled, all things would be known
All things would be enjoyed, fulfilled, and come to be my own.

How like a summer the years of youth have passed!
—How like the summer of 1914, in all truth!—
Patience, my soul, the truth is never known
Until the future has become the past
And then, only, when the love of truth at last
Becomes the truth of love, when both are one,
Then, then, then, Eden becomes Utopia and is surpassed:
For then the dream of knowledge and knowledge knows
Motive and joy at once wherever it goes.

I Am a Book I neither Wrote nor Read

I am a book I neither wrote nor read,
A comic, tragic play in which new masquerades
Astonishing as guns crackle like raids
Newly each time, whatever one is prepared
To come upon, suddenly dismayed and afraid,
As in the dreams which make the fear of sleep
The terror of love, the depth one cannot leap.

How the false truths of the years of youth have passed!
Have passed at full speed like trains which never stopped
There where I stood and waited, hardly aware,
How little I knew, or which of them was the one
To mount and ride to hope or where true hope arrives.

I no more wrote than read that book which is
The self I am, half-hidden as it is
From one and all who see within a kiss
The lounging formless blackness of an abyss.

How could I think the brief years were enough
To prove the reality of endless love?

The Conclusion

How slow time moves when torment stops the clock!
How dormant and delinquent, under the dawn,
The uproarious roaring of the bursting cock:
Now pain ticks on, now all and nothing must be borne,
And I remember: pain is the cost of being born.

2

For when the flowers of infatuation fade
The furs which love in all its warmth discloses
Become the fires of pride and are betrayed
By those whom love has terrified and pride has made afraid.

No matter what time prepares, no matter how time amazes
The images and hopes by which we love or die,
Pride is not love, and pride is merely pride,
Until it becomes a living death which denies
How it is treacherous, and faithless: how it betrays
Everyone, one by one, and every vow,
Seeking praise absolute, hides with other whores
Whom pride and time seduces and love ignores.

3

This will be true long after heart and heart
Have recognized and forgotten all that was ripening, ripe, rotten-ripe
    and rotten:
Have known too soon, too soon by far how much of love has been
    forgotten:
Have known the little deaths before death do us part:
Nothing will ever pass at last to nothingness beyond decay
Until the night is all, and night is known all day.

The Sequel

First love is first death. There is no other.
There is no death. But all men live forever
And die forever. If this were not true,
We would be more deceived, still more deceived
Than this belief deceives us, whether or not
We think that we believe or we think
Those who believe are deceived. But to believe
That death is the sweet asylum of nothingness:
Is the cruel sick dream of the criminal and the suicide:
Of those who deny reality, of those who steal from consciousness,
Of those who are often fugitive, of those who are afraid to live,
Of those who are terrified by love, and
        Those who try—before they
            Try to die—to disappear
                And hide.

The Dark and Falling Summer

The rain was full of the freshness
    and the fresh fragrance of darkening grapes,
The rain was as the dark falling of hidden
And fabulous grapes ripening, great blue thunderheads moving slowly,
    slowly blooming.
The dark air was possessed by the fragrance of freshness,
By a scattered and confused profusion until
After the tattering began, the pouring down came
And plenitude descended, multitudinous:
Everywhere was full of the pulsing of the loud and fallen dark.

That time of year you may in me behold
When Christmas trees are blazing on the walk,
Raging against stale snow and the cold
And low sky's bundled wash, deadwhite as chalk.

Hissing and ravenous the brilliant plant:
Rising like eagerness, a rushing pyre
(As when the *tutti* foams up and the chant
Soars up—hurrahing!—from the Easter choir).

But this is only true at four o'clock.

At noon the fifth year is again abused:
I bring a distant girl apples and cake,
Marbles, pictures, secrets, my swollen heart
Now boxed in the learning and music of art:

But once more, as before, accepted and refused.

All of the fruits had fallen,
The bears had fallen asleep,
And the pears were useless and soft
Like used hopes, under the starlight's
Small knowledge, scattered aloft
In a glittering senseless drift:
The jackals of remorse in a cage
Drugged beyond mirth and rage.

Then, then, the dark hour flowered!
Under the silence, immense
And empty as far-off seas,
I wished for the innocence
Of my stars and my stones and my trees
All the brutality and inner sense
A dog and a bird possess,
The dog who barked at the moon
As an enemy's white fang,
The bird that thrashed up the bush
And soared to soar as it sang,
A being all present as touch,
Free of the future and past
—Until, in the dim window glass,
The fog or cloud of my face
Showed me my fear at last!

When I was a young man, I loved to write poems
    And I called a spade a spade
And the only only thing that made me sing
    Was to lift the masks at the masquerade.
I took them off my own face,
    I took them off others too
And the only only wrong in all my song
    Was the view that I knew what was true.

Now I am older and tireder too
    And the tasks with the masks are quite trying.
I'd gladly gladly stop if I only only knew
    A better way to keep from lying,
And not get nervous and blue
    When I said something quite untrue:
I looked all around and all over
    To find something else to do:
I tried to be less romantic
    I tried to be less starry-eyed too:
But I only got mixed up and frantic
    Forgetting what was false and what was true.

But tonight I am going to the masked ball,
    Because it has occurred to me
That the masks are more true than the faces:
    —Perhaps this too is poetry?
I no longer yearn to be naïve and stern
    And masked balls fascinate me:
Now that I know that most falsehoods are true
    Perhaps I can join the charade?
This is, at any rate, my new and true view:
    Let live and believe, I say.
The only only thing is to believe in everything:
    It's more fun and safer that way!

I Did Not Know the Truth of Growing Trees

On the suburban street, guarded by patient trees
Two family houses huddled. As I passed the lamplight's teas,
In the mid-winter evening when the snow's light made
Of the glowing supper hour a blue lost shade:
A blond girl stood at the window and looked toward the snow:
Her glance hid hatred's hot-bed, which had sickened long ago,
And then our glances met: and I fell suddenly,
My eyes reached to touch the bark of the nearest tree,
My hands stretched to touch the rough and broken
Bark to feel, again and again, in instance and a token
Of reality's texture. The picture window showed
How often beauty conceals the heart's diseased death-ridden toad:
How often romance is a passing dance: but the tree is true:
And this is what I did not know, although I always thought I knew
   how a growing tree is true.

All of them are fixed, although each has gone away,
Eva and Sinbad, dead these seven years,
Betty and Mrs. Muller, heroines in a play,
Which has not been performed: the soul is in arrears
To all that touch it slightly or ring it like a bell,
For once they have departed, I stand as on a roof
And see them as they were then, troubled and unwell,
For all these things are still now and now I am aloof
Not anxious, nor impetuous, not nervous, but free,
Knowing the past unalterable, and that it must now be
Like the sun in the sky and the sun in the great unsettled forever
    drunken sea!

I Did Not Know the Spoils of Joy

When that I was and a little tiny boy,
    With a hey ho, the wind and the rain.
I did not know the truth of joy:
    I thought that life was passed in pain.

Then, when I came to thought and art,
    The flowers of hope began to wilt:
I glowed disgusted with my heart,
    As cynicism salved my guilt.

When youthful hopes proved true and false,
    As hard-earned riches fade and pall,
I thought the mind lied like a waltz
    Which chants love as a brilliant ball.

And when I followed where sleep fled
    I woke amid the mixing dream:
My self or others hurt my head,
    I heard the frigid Furies scream.

Yet, when I fled from this estate,
    I drove the quickest car to bliss:
With drunken fools I struck at fate,
    Charmed, by the falls of consciousness.

A great while ago the world began,
    With a ho ho, the fog and the mist,
The Pharaohs are in power again,
    The endless wind and rain persist.

Illusion and madness dim the years:
    Mere parodies of hope, at best,
And yet, through all these mounting fears,
    How I am glad that I exist!

For now I know the spoils of joy:
I only knew the spells of joy.

How strange the truth appears at last!
I feel as old as wornout shoes:
I know what I have lost or missed,
Or certainly will some day lose
I know the follies whom I kissed,
Whom self-deception will accuse——

And yet this knowledge, like the Jews,
Can make me glad that I exist!
Although I must my self accuse
Not when I win, but when I lose:
Although this knowledge comes and goes,
Although the wind and the rain persist:
How I am glad that I exist!
    With a hey ho, the stupid past,
        And a ho ho, a ha ha and a hurrah at last.

I Waken to a Calling

I waken to a calling,
A calling from somewhere down, from a great height,
Calling out of pleasure and happiness,
And out of darkness, like a new light,
A delicate ascending voice,
Which seems forever rising, never falling
Telling all of us to rejoice,
To delight in the darkness and the light,
Commanding all consciousness forever to rejoice!

As I looked, the poplar rose in the shining air
Like a slender throat,
And there was an exaltation of flowers,
The surf of apple tree delicately foaming.

All winter, the trees had been
Silent soldiers, a vigil of woods,
Their hidden feelings
Scrawled and became
Scores of black vines,
Barbed wire sharp against the ice-white sky.
Who could believe then
In the green, glittering vividness of full-leafed summer?
Who will be able to believe, when winter again begins
After the autumn burns down again, and the day is ashen,
And all returns to winter and winter's ashes,
Wet, white, ice, wooden, dulled and dead, brittle or frozen,
Who will believe or feel in mind and heart
The reality of the spring and of birth,
In the green warm opulence of summer, and the inexhaustible vitality
    and immortality of the earth?

"Outside the cicadas are singing fit to burst, a harsh screech-
ing, ten times stronger than crickets, and the scorched grass
takes on the lovely tones of old gold."

VAN GOGH, Letter to his brother.

All through the brilliant blue and gold afternoon
All space was blossoming: immense and stately against the blue
heights
The sailing, summer-swollen milky and mounting clouds: colossal
blossoms,
And the dark statues of the trees on the blue and green ground,
flowing. And every solid thing
Moved as in bloom, leafing, opening wing upon wing to the sun's
overwhelming lightning!
And every solid sight was a great green drum, throbbing and pulsing
in the growing vividness of the greenness darkening
So that the litter and ripple of the river was excited by the advent and
descent of light upon its slow flowing:
The river was opulence, radiance, sparkle, and shine, a rippling radiance dancing light's dances;
And the birds flew, soared, darted, perched, perched and whistled,
dipped or ascended
Like a ballet of black flutes, an erratic and scattered metamorphosis
of the villages of stillness into the variety of flying:
The birds were as a transformation of trunk and branch and twig into
the elation which is the energy's celebration and consummation!

—It was difficult, then, to believe—how difficult it was and how painful it was to believe in the reality of winter,
Beholding so many supple somersaults of energy and deathless feats
of superexuberant vitality, all self-delighting,
Arising, waving, flying, glittering, and glistening as if in irresistible
eagerness,

Seeking with serene belief and undivided certainty, love's miracles,
tender, or thrashing, or thrashing towards tenderness boldly.
   It was necessary to think of pine and fir,
      Of holly, ivy, barberry bush and icicle, of frozen ground,
         And of wooden tree, white or wet and drained,
         And of the blackened or stiffened arms of elm, oak and maple
      To remember, even a little, that existence was not forever
         May and the beginning of summer:
It was only possible to forget the presence of the present's green and
   gold and white flags of flowering May's victory, summer's ascend-
   ancy and sovereignty,
By thinking of how all arise and aspire to the nature of fire, to the
   flame-like climbing of vine and leaf and flower,
And calling to mind how all things must suffer and die in growth and
   birth,
To be reborn, again and again and again, to be transformed all over
   again.

The desire of the bud and the flower and the fruit the tree and the
   vine to be devoured and to be phoenix in nature, fulfilled in the
   phoenix sensuality of blood and of wine, or stilled in the mud near
   the root under the ground once more awaiting the sun's domination, the sun's great roar and fire.

How strange love is in every kind of consciousness:
How strange it is that only such gentleness
Begets the fury of joy and all its tenderness,
That lips and hands for all their littleness
Can move throughout the body's wilderness
Beyond the gaze of consciousness, however it towers
Possessed and blessed by the power which flowers as a fountain
    flowers!

The Mounting Summer, Brilliant and Ominous

A yellow-headed, gold-hammered, sunflower-lanterned
Summer afternoon: after the sun soared
All morning to the marble-shining heights of the marvellous blue
Like lions insurgent, bursting out of a great black zoo,
As if all radiance rode over and roved and dove
To the thick dark night where the fluted roots clutched and grasped
As if all vividness poured, out poured
Over, bursting and falling and breaking,
As when the whole ocean rises and rises, in irresistible, uncontrollable
    motion, shaking:
The roar of the heart in a shell and the roar of the sea beyond the
    concessions of possession and the successions of time's continual
    procession.

The afternoon turned dark early;
The light suddenly faded;
The dusk was black although, elsewhere, the first star in the cold sky
    suddenly whistled,
And I thought I heard the fresh scraping of the flying steel of boys on
    roller skates
Rollicking over the asphalt in 1926,
And I thought I heard the dusk and silence raided
By a calm voice commanding consciousness:
Wait: wait: wait as if you had always waited
And as if it had always been dark
And as if the world had been from the beginning
A lost and drunken ark in which the only light
Was the dread and white of the terrified animals' eyes.
And then, turning on the light, I took a book
That I might gaze upon another's vision of the abyss of conscious-
    ness—
The hope, and the pain of hope, and the patience of hope and its
    torment, its astonishment, its endlessness.

A *Dream of Winter, Empty, Woolen, Ice-White and Brittle*

The leaden sky of winter whitened, brightened a little
By what is hidden and beyond it now, became a luminous
Grey, as if the color of smoke curtained the fire
Which was open and offered freely all through the halcyon
Summer, blue and gold—when the great blond and yellow light blazed
    and imagined or implied
Infinite hope, endless love—as promise? as abyss?
    as the depth of absolute loss
    where every heart is lost at last?
The angel or the star which wakened the eye to consciousness
Whispered new intimations, and forgotten truth, concealed and am-
    biguous,
In the ultimate box-seat and balcony of the blue: "You
Were what you are not now, now you are what you were not, and
    you are
Open and ever-ripening and far less than you may become or be
Within the future's bewildering reality:
Then perhaps you will be a new and astonishing, undreamed actuality:
And then, surely, you will be far different and other
Than the half-believed, half-deceived, revery and lyric of your gaz-
    ing, gaping, grasping, flickering, fumbling desperate and possessed
    memory!"

In the green morning, before
Love was destiny,
The sun was king,
And God was famous.

The merry, the musical,
The jolly, the magical,
The feast, the feast of feasts, the festival
Suddenly ended
As the sky descended
But there was only the feeling,
In all the dark falling,
Of fragrance and of freshness, of birth and beginning.

8

THE
PHOENIX CHOIR

Once and for All

Once, when I was a boy,
Apollo summoned me
To be apprenticed to the endless summer of light and consciousness,
And thus to become and be what poets often have been,
A shepherd of being, a riding master of being, holding the sun-god's
    horses, leading his sheep, training his eagles,
Directing the constellations to their stations, and to each grace of
    place.
But the goat-god, piping and dancing, speaking an unknown tongue
    or the language of the magician,
Sang from the darkness or rose from the underground, whence arise
Love and love's drunkenness, love and birth, love and death, death
    and rebirth
Which are the beginning of the phoenix festivals, the tragic plays in
    celebration of Dionysus,
And in mourning for his drunken and fallen princes, the singers and
    sinners, fallen because they are, in the end,
Drunken with pride, blinded by joy.

And I followed Dionysus, forgetting Apollo. I followed him far too
    long until I was wrong and chanted:
"One cannot serve both gods. One must choose to win and lose."
But I was wrong and when I knew how I was wrong I knew
What, in a way, I had known all along:
This was the new world, here I belonged, here I was wrong because
Here every tragedy has a happy ending, and any error may be
A fabulous discovery of America, of the opulence hidden in the dark
    depths and glittering heights of reality.

Cupid is
    The king of flutes.
Cupid's kiss
    Wakes winter's roots.
Cupid touches
    A color's curve.
Cupid reaches
    Apples, peaches,
        Eye and nerve.

A tutor of Venus
        In the dark of the sun,
He knows and he teaches
        That the clever are stupid
        For the stupid discover
How sleep and love are warm and one.

2

Cupid is
A student of leaves,
A scholar of Eros,
A savant of consciousness,
And of sleep's wine-dark seas;
Of the heights of the birds
And the insides of words,
The seed within Adam,
The birth, the death, and the rebirth
Which breathes in Eve
—All that is seedy, loamy, rising, fickle, growing, seeking, flowing,
    flowering, and unknowable, all that we hope and hardly dare to
    believe.

O heart, O dearest heart, dusk again becomes black night
As quickly as the falling of a leave: and I am left
Fondling the formless faceless presence I love, quite lost:
—All that I am is seed, all that I am is morning, waiting to see,
All that I am is flower, forbidden the light and hidden
In sleep's purpose and sleep's patience, power and growth:
So I must ask again, knowing how it angers you
And knowing that you would be more angered if you knew
How much this mostly unasked question obsesses me:
Why is love dark?
Why must your face remain concealed from me?
My sisters taunt and torment me. They say
I have invented a religion, a superstition, a deity
To hide the love of a monster or monstrous usages
Nursed by love's absence, love's unquelled desire.
Must you be hidden from me forever?
My sisters sometimes say that I will never see
The strangeness or the strange face of the deity
To whom I am espoused in reality or in the dark forest of fantasy!

Does your face possess the glitter and radiance
Possessed by your voice? Your voice possesses
A bell clarity, a trumpet brilliance, a harpsichord delicacy.
It is blessed by the gentleness of the first morning, exquisitely!
Sometimes it has a sunset's roaring eloquence and turbulence
. . . Yet my sisters laugh at me. And think of me
As one who is very strange, as one possessed
By lunacy, or by a dream dispossessed, when in all blessedness
—By joy overcome, beside myself, outside myself, in ecstasy's after-
    math—
I come and say to them that God has captured and kidnapped me!
Dearest, is all love dark? Must all love be
Hidden in night from the one who is nearest?

Or is the mystery of divinity an abyss of black?
How then can you come to me? why do you come back?
Why do you desire my love? Is it love, in truth, if I lack
The sight and vision which begins all intimacy?

Narcissus

THE MIND IS AN ANCIENT AND FAMOUS CAPITAL

The mind is a city like London,
Smoky and populous: it is a capital
Like Rome, ruined and eternal,
Marked by the monuments which no one
Now remembers. For the mind, like Rome, contains
Catacombs, aqueducts, amphitheatres, palaces,
Churches and equestrian statues, fallen, broken or soiled.
The mind possesses and is possessed by all the ruins
Of every haunted, hunted generation's celebration.

"Call us what you will: we are made such by love."
We are such studs as dreams are made on, and
Our little lives are ruled by the gods, by Pan,
Piping of all, seeking to grasp or grasping
All of the grapes; and by the bow-and-arrow god,
Cupid, piercing the heart through, suddenly and forever.

Dusk we are, to dusk returning, after the burbing,
After the gold fall, the fallen ash, the bronze,
Scattered and rotten, after the white null statues which
Are winter, sleep, and nothingness: when
Will the houselights of the universe
Light up and blaze?
                    For it is not the sea
Which murmurs in a shell,
And it is not only heart, at harp o'clock,
It is the dread terror of the uncontrollable
Horses of the apocalypse, running in wild dread
Toward Arcturus—and returning as suddenly . . .

—The others were the despots of despair—

The river's freshness sailed from unknown sources—

. . . They snickered giggled, laughed aloud at last,
They mocked and marvelled at the statue which was
A caricature, as strained and stiff, and yet
A statue of self-love!—since self-love was
To them, truly my true love, how, then, was I a stillness of nervousness
So nervous a caricature: did they suppose
Self-love was unrequited, or betrayed?
They thought I had fallen in love with my own face,
And this belief became the night-like obstacle
To understanding all my unbroken suffering,
My studious self-regard, the pain of hope,
The torment of possibility:
How then could I have expected them to see me
As I saw myself, within my gaze, or see
That being thus seemed as a toad, a frog, a wen, a mole.
Knowing their certainty that I was only
A monument, a monster who had fallen in love
With himself alone, how could I have
Told them what was in me, within my heart, trembling and passionate
Within the labyrinth and caves of my mind, which is
Like every mind partly or wholly hidden from itself?
The words for what is in my heart and in my mind
Do not exist. But I must seek and search to find
Amid the vines and orchards of the vivid world of day
Approximate images, imaginary parallels
For what is my heart and dark within my mind:
Comparisons and mere metaphors: for all
Of them are substitutes, both counterfeit and vague:

They are, at most, deceptive resemblances,
False in their very likeness, like the sons
Who are alike and kin and more unlike and false
Because they seem the father's very self: but each one is
—Although begotten by the same forbears—himself,
The unique self, each one is unique, like every other one,
And everything, older or younger, nevertheless
A passionate nonesuch who has before has been.
Do you hear, do you see? Do you understand me now, and how
The words for what is my heart do not exist?

THE RIVER WAS THE EMBLEM OF ALL BEAUTY: ALL

. . .
The river was the abundant belly of beauty itself
The river was the dream space where I walked,
The river was itself and yet it was—flowing and freshening—
A self anew, another self, or self renewed
At every tick of eternity, and by each glint of light
Mounting or sparkling, descending to shade and black
—Had I but told them my heart, told how it was
Taunted at noon and pacified at dusk, at starfall midnight
Strong in hope once more, ever in eagerness
Jumping like joy, would they have heard? How could they?
How, when what they knew was, like the grass,
Simple and certain, known through the truth of touch, another form
      and fountain of falsehood's fecundity——
Gazing upon their faces as they gazed
Could they have seen my faces as whores who are
Holy and deified as priestesses of hope
                  —the sacred virgins of futurity—
Promising dear divinity precisely because
They were disfigured ducks who might become
And be, and ever beloved, white swans, noble and beautiful.
                  Could they have seen how my faces were

Bonfires of worship and vigil, blazes of adoration and hope
—Surely they would have laughed again, renewed their scorn,
Giggled and snickered, cruel. Surely have said
This is the puerile mania of the obsessed,
The living logic of the lunatic:
I was the statue of their merriment,
Dead and a death, Pharoah and monster forsaken and lost.

. . .
My faces were my apes: my apes became
Performers in the Sundays of their parks,
Buffoons or clowns in the farce or comedy
When they took pleasure in knowing that they were not like me.

. . .
I waited like obsession in solitude:
The sun's white terror tore and roared at me,
The moonlight, almond white, at night,
Whether awake or sleeping, arrested me
And sang, softly, haunted, unlike the sun
But as the sun. Withheld from me or took away
Despair or peace, making me once more
With thought of what had never been before——

Abraham

To J. M. Kaplan

I was a mere boy in a stone-cutter's shop
When, early one evening, my raised hand
Was halted and the soundless voice said:
"Depart from your father and your country
And the things to which you are accustomed.
Go now into a country unknown and strange
I will make of your children a great nation,
Your generations will haunt every generation of all the nations,
They will be like the stars at midnight, like the sand of the sea."
Then I looked up at the infinite sky,
Star-pointing and silent, and it was then, on that evening, that I
Became a man: that evening of my manhood's birthday.

I went then to Egypt, the greatest of nations.
There I encountered the Pharaoh who built the tombs,
Great public buildings, many theatres, and seashore villas:
And my wife's beauty was such that, fearing his power and lust,
I called her my sister, a girl neither for him nor for me.
And soon was fugitive, a nomad again.
Living alone with my sister, becoming very rich
In all but children, in herds, in possessions, the herds continually
Increased my possessions through prodigies of progeny.

From time to time, in the afternoon's revery
In the late sunlight or the cool of the evening
I called to mind the protracted vanity of that promise
Which had called me forth from my father's house unwillingly
Into the last strangeness of Egypt and the childless desert.
Then Sarah gave me her handmaid, a young girl
That I might at least at last have children by another
And later, when a great deal else had occurred,
I put away Hagar, with the utmost remorse
Because the child was the cause of so much rivalry and jealousy.

At last when all this had passed or when
The promise seemed the parts of dream,
When we were worn out and patient in all things
The stranger came, suave and elegant,
A messenger who renewed the promise, making Sarah
Burst out laughing hysterically!

But the boy was born and grew and I saw
What I had known, I knew what I had seen, for he
Possessed his mother's beauty and his father's humility,
And was not marked and marred by her sour irony and my endless
    anxiety.

Then the angel returned, asking that I surrender
My son as a lamb to show that humility
Still lived in me, and was not altered by age and prosperity.

I said nothing, shocked and passive. Then I said but to myself alone:
"This was to be expected. These promises
Are never unequivocal or unambiguous, in this
As in all things which are desired the most:
I have had great riches and great beauty.
I cannot expect the perfection of every wish
And if I deny the command, who knows what will happen?"

But his life was forgiven and given back to me:
His children and their children are an endless nation:
Dispersed on every coast. And I am not gratified
Nor astonished. It has never been otherwise:
Exiled, wandering, dumbfounded by riches,
Estranged among strangers, dismayed by the infinite sky,
An alien to myself until at last the caste of the last alienation
The angel of death comes to make the alienated and indestructible
    one a part of his famous society.

Sarah

The angel said to me: "Why are you laughing?"
"Laughing! Not me! Who was laughing? I did not laugh. It was
A cough. I was coughing. Only hyenas laugh.
It was the cold I caught nine minutes after
Abraham married me: when I saw
How I was slender and beautiful, more and more
Slender and beautiful.
       I was also
Clearing my throat; something inside of me
Is continually telling me something
I do not wish to hear: A joke: A big joke:
But the joke is always just on me.
He said: you will have more children than the sky's stars
And the seashore's sands, if you just wait patiently.
Wait: patiently: ninety years? You see
The joke's on me!"

Jacob

All was as it is, before the beginning began, before
We were bared to the cold air, before
Pride. Fullness of bread. Abundance of idleness.
No one has ever told me what now I know:
Love is unjust, justice is loveless.

So, as it was to become, it was, in the black womb's ignorance
Coiled and bound, under the mother's heart.
There in the womb we wrestled, and writhed, hurt
Each other long before each was other and apart,
Before we breathed: who then committed greed,
Impersonation, usurpation? So, in the coming forth,
In the noose and torment of birth, Esau went first,
He was red all over. I followed him, clutching his heel,
And we were named: Esau, the one of the vivid coat,
Jacob, the one who clutches the heel of the one
Who has a vivid coat. The names were true
As the deceptive reality into which we were thrown.
For I did not know what clutching was, nor had I known
Would I have known whose heel I clutched, my brother's or my own!

So, the world we entered then and thus was one
In which the second must be second that the first may be first.
The world of precedence, order, other, under and above,
The darkness, sweetness, confusion and unity of love!
How the truth of our names became, as we grew, more true,
Growing like truth. How could it be otherwise? For truth abides
Hidden in the future, in the ambush of the marvellous,
Unknown and monstrous, at the very heart of surprise.

The gift was mind. The gift was eminence. The gift
Like every gift, was guilt. The guilt began
In the darkness and dark mystery where all begins.
The mystery of the perpetual invisible fires whence flow

The very beasts and woods where—
                    with what happiness!
                    what innocence!—
Esau my brother hunted, cantering like the horses of summer,
And sleeping, when he returned, the sleep of winter farms,
Spontaneous and blessed, like energy itself, sleeping or awake.
Until the hour when the angel struck!

So it was: so:
O angel of the unspeakable,
Why must a gift be guilt and hurt the gifted one?
O angel of the unspeakable, power of powers,
Locking my reins, my arms, my heart all night
So that my body was burdened as with the load of all stones
Dost thou remember what, in the darkness, I cried,
During the desperation in which I died
The last death of hope and the little deaths of the heart
Wrestling and writhing between two rivers—on one bank,
Esau, awaiting me, like a river slept—beneath me once more.
"Hast thou not seen," I cried aloud, to the unspeakable,
"Esau my brother: his handsome hunting heart upon a horse?"
How should it seem so strange that I should win,
Since victory was my gift? Unjust, like every gift,
A something neither deserved, nor gained by toil . . .
How else could it be gift and given?
Favor: favored: favorite:
Gold hair: great strength: Esau was very tall,
Possessed by the supple grace of the sea's waves, breaking.

Now Joseph is, as I was: in Egypt's pit,
In that accustomed depth and isolated height
The solitude of eminence, the exiled intelligence,
Which separated me even as it created me:
Estranged and unloved, gifted and detested,
Denied the love of the servants and the dogs.
Joseph a stranger in Egypt may only know
What I have known: my gifts, my victory, my guilt.
For Egypt is a country like a gift.

The gift is loved but not the gifted one.
The coat of many colors is much admired
By everyone, but he who wears the coat
Is not made warm. Why should the gift be the cause of pain,
O thou unspeakable? Must the vivid coat
Of eminence elect the favored favorite
As scapegoat or turncoat, exile or fugitive,
The loved of mother and God, and by all others
Shunned in fear or contempt?
                              I knew what it was,
When Joseph became my favorite: knew the sympathy
Of the long experience of the unasked-for gift:
Knew the nature of love: how many colors
Can a coat have? What should we wish, if
We could choose? What should I desire
—Not to have loved my son, the best of sons?
Rejected the choice of love? Should I have hidden
My love of him? Or should he have concealed the self
I loved, above all others, wearing the coat
Which is customary, the coats his brothers wore?
To how many coats can a color give vividness?
How can the heart know love, and not love one the more?
Love is unjust: justice is loveless.

Lincoln

Manic-depressive Lincoln, national hero!
How just and true that this great nation, being conceived
In liberty by fugitives should find
—Strange ways and plays of monstrous History—
This Hamlet-type to be the President—

This failure, this unwilling bridegroom,
This tricky lawyer full of black despair—

He grew a beard, becoming President,
And took a shawl as if he guessed his role,
Though with the beard he fled cartoonists' blacks,
And many laughed and were contemptuous,
And some for four years spoke of killing him—

He was a politician—of the heart!—
He lived from hand to mouth in moral things!
He understood quite well Grant's drunkenness!
It was for him, before Election Day,
That at Cold Harbor Grant threw lives away
In hopeless frontal attack against Lee's breastworks!

O how he was the Hamlet-man, and this,
After a life of failure made him right,
After he ran away on his wedding day,
Writing a coward's letter to his bride—
How with his very failure, he out-tricked
The florid Douglas and the abstract Davis,
And all the vain men who, surrounding him,
Smiled in their vanity and sought his place—

Later, they made him out a prairie Christ
To sate the need coarse in the national heart—

His wife went insane, Mary Todd too often

Bought herself dresses. And his child died.
And he would not condemn young men to death
For having slept, in weakness. And he spoke
More than he knew and all that he had felt
Between outrageous joy and black despair
Before and after Gettysburg's pure peak—

He studied law, but knew in his own soul
Despair's anarchy, terror and error,
—Instruments had to be taken from his office
And from his bedroom in such days of horror,
Because some saw that he might kill himself:
When he was young, when he was middle-aged,
How just and true was he, our national hero!

Sometimes he could not go home to face his wife,
Sometimes he wished to hurry or end his life!
But do not be deceived. He did not win,
And, it is plain, the South could never win
(Despite the gifted Northern generals!)
—Capitalismus is not mocked, O no!
This stupid deity decided the War—

In fact, the North and South were losers both:
—Capitalismus won the Civil War—

—Capitalismus won the Civil War,
Yet, in the War's cruel Colosseum,
Some characters fulfilled their natures' surds,
Grant the drunkard, Lee the noble soldier,
John Brown in whom the Bible soared and cried,
Booth the unsuccessful Shakespearean,
—Each in some freedom walked and knew himself,
Then most of all when all the deities
Mixed with their barbarous stupidity
To make the rock, root, and rot of the war—

"This is the way each only life becomes,
Tossed on History's ceaseless insane sums!"

The starlight's intuitions pierced the twelve,
The brittle night sky sparkled like a tune
Tinkled and tapped out on the xylophone.
Empty and vain, a glittering dune, the moon
Arose too big, and, in the mood which ruled,
Seemed like a useless beauty in a pit;
And then one said, after he carefully spat:
"No matter what we do, he looks at it!

"I cannot see a child or find a girl
Beyond his smile which glows like that spring moon."
"—Nothing no more the same," the second said,
"Though all may be forgiven, never quite healed
The wound I bear as witness, standing by;
No ceremony surely appropriate,
Nor secret love, escape or sleep because
No matter what I do, he looks at it——"

"Now," said the third, "no thing will be the same:
I am as one who never shuts his eyes,
The sea and sky no more are marvellous,
And I no longer understand surprise!"
"Now," said the fourth, "nothing will be enough
—I heard his voice accomplishing all wit:
No word can be unsaid, no deed withdrawn
—No matter what is said, he measures it!"

"Vision, imagination, hope or dream,
Believed, denied, the scene we wished to see?
It does not matter in the least: for what
Is altered, if it is not true? That we
Saw goodness, as it is—*this* is the awe
And the abyss which we will not forget,

His story now the sky which holds all thought:
No matter what I think, think of it!"

"And I will never be what once I was,"
Said one for long as narrow as a knife,
"And we will never be what once we were;
We have died once; this is a second life."
"My mind is spilled in moral chaos," one
Righteous as Job exclaimed, "now infinite
Suspicion of my heart stems what I will
—No matter what I choose, he stares at it!"

"I am as one native in summer places
—Ten weeks' excitement paid for by the rich;
Debauched by that and then all winter bored,"
The sixth declared. "His peak left us a ditch!"
"He came to make this life more difficult,"
The seventh said, "No one will ever fit
His measure's heights, all is inadequate:
No matter what I do, what good is it?"

"He gave forgiveness to us: what a gift!"
The eighth chimed in. "But now we know how much
Must be forgiven. But if forgiven, what?
The crime which was will be; and the least touch
Revives the memory: what is forgiveness worth?"
The ninth spoke thus: "Who now will ever sit
At ease in Zion at the Easter feast?
No matter what the place, he touches it!"

"And I will always stammer, since he spoke,"
One, who had been most eloquent, said, stammering.
"I looked too long at the sun; like too much light,
So too much goodness is a boomerang,"
Laughed the eleventh of the troop. "I must
Try what he tried: I saw the infinite
Who walked the lake and raised the hopeless dead:
No matter what the feat, he first accomplished it!"

So spoke the twelfth; and then the twelve in chorus:
"Unspeakable unnatural goodness is
Risen and shines, and never will ignore us;
He glows forever in all consciousness;
Forgiveness, love, and hope possess the pit,
And bring our endless guilt, like shadow's bars:
No matter what we do, he stares at it!

What pity then deny? what debt defer?
We know he looks at us like all the stars,
And we shall never be as once we were,
This life will never be what once it was!"

A